Decorating & Craft Ideas

for

Christmas 1983

BY

SHELLEY STEWART

JO VOCE

OXMOOR HOUSE INC.
BIRMINGHAM

CONTENTS

INTRODUCTION

INTRODUCTION

Christmas is the magical season, viewed through a happy haze of treasured memories and fond anticipations. The sights and sounds. The flurry of activity. The homemade goodies. The friendly get-togethers. The gift that you cannot wait to give. . .

Celebrate Christmas, and store up happy memories for the future, by putting your talents and the love you feel for your family into action. This book is designed to help you stretch your time and make your money go farther—with page after page of novel decorating ideas to give your home a festive appearance and with dozens of appealing gifts and holiday crafts that you can make.

There are ornaments and wreaths, placemats and centerpieces, tree skirts and table skirts, and a host of other decorations involving more imagination than money. These are often made with materials you already have around the house or from natural materials that are free for the gathering.

You will enjoy using your hands to make gifts and crafts for both friends and family. There are enough projects to paint, sculpt, glue, fold, embroider, snip, and stitch to keep you pleasantly busy for months—but there are also ideas for gifts that take only a few minutes to complete. Your children will be able to help with many of the simpler projects, and, in doing so, they will learn to know that special pride that comes from making a gift yourself.

Directions are written in clear, straightforward language, and full-size patterns are given for most of the projects. Ideas that are either low-cost or no-cost, or which provide a big effect for relatively little money, are marked with this easy-to-spot symbol—a snowflake.

There is also a section of the most delectable holiday foods ever to grace a table, organized into menus so that you may plan the occasion with confidence. Whether you are serving a make-ahead brunch to your relatives on Christmas morning, ladling steaming soup for a crowd of hungry carolers, or whipping up an absolutely outrageous dessert for a Twelfth Night party, you are sure to find recipes that you enjoy. Some may even become such favorites that your family requests them in years to come.

In short, this book is a time-saving, money-saving aid to help you make the most of the season. By using your skills to create some of the ideas given on these pages and adding your own loving touches, you may give your family the best gift of all, their merriest Christmas ever!

CROSS-STITCH AN HEIRLOOM

Tasteful and elegant on a buffet, yet as comfortably old-fashioned as your grandmother's dresser scarf—this table runner has the timeless appeal of an heirloom-to-be. The runner is worked in counted cross-stitch on a background of white, with a large motif of richly colored poinsettia flowers and leaves in the center and a Greek key design at each corner. The same design might be worked in the center of a large tablecloth or on an individual placemat. A single flower might even be worked on the bib of a matching hostess apron.

YOU WILL NEED:
chart and color key on pages 126 and 127
#11 white Aida cloth (17" x 41" piece)
#24 blunt tapestry needle
embroidery flosses in colors shown in the color key

Do not preshrink the fabric. To finish the edges, turn under each raw edge ¼" and press; then turn under again ¼", press again, and machine stitch ⅛" from the folded outer edge of the runner.

Locate the exact center of the Aida cloth by folding it carefully end to end and side to side, pressing a crease into the fabric along each fold. Hand baste through existing holes along these creases, using a contrasting thread; you need to baste only 6" on each side of the center along the lengthwise crease. (Be careful to follow the same row of holes across the fabric.) The point where the two lines intersect is the exact center. Note that the poinsettia design is stitched twice, once on each side of the center line. (See photograph.)

Work the design in cross-stitch. Each of the figured squares on the chart equals one cross-stitch, and squares which are left plain represent the cloth as is. All parts of the design are worked with two strands of floss. When the embroidery is finished, pull out the basting threads marking the center. Hand wash the fabric in cold water with mild soap, rinsing until the water is clear. Blot and drip dry, but do not wring. Press on the wrong side with a steam iron. The runner will have shrunk from ½" to ¾" in both length and width.

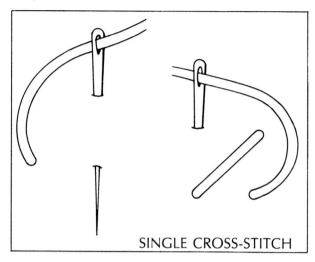

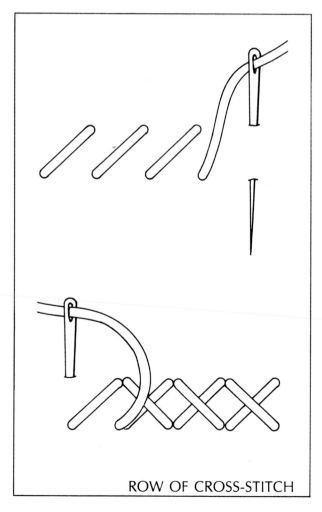

SINGLE CROSS-STITCH

ROW OF CROSS-STITCH

2

A WINTER FLOORCLOTH

When temperatures drop, curl up in front of the fire and warm your toes on a painted canvas floorcloth. Its sturdy surface protects the area in front of the hearth from flying sparks and bits of soot, yet it wipes clean with just a damp sponge.

Not only is the floorcloth useful; its bright design adds a pleasant accent to the room. The forest of evergreens in drifts of fallen snow is surrounded by a painted calico border—all in country-fresh colors. When winter is over, roll the canvas and store in a cool, dry place until next year.

YOU WILL NEED:
patterns on page 128
medium-weight canvas (26" x 38") either primed or unprimed
gesso (only if using unprimed canvas)
liquid latex or flexible glue
white semi-gloss latex paint (background)
acetate or stencil paper
craft knife
stencil brush
acrylic paints (medium blue, 2 shades of green, gold, red, white)
polyurethane varnish (glossy or satin)

Purchase either unprimed canvas at a shop making awnings or primed canvas at an art supply store. Cut the canvas to the proper size, priming it if necessary with one coat of gesso. Allow to dry. Fold under 1" all around for the hem, mitering the corners. Press with an iron to make sharp creases at the edges; then glue in place with liquid latex or other flexible glue. Allow to dry.

Brush the entire background with one coat of white latex paint. When this dries, measure and mark with pencil a border 3" from each edge. Mark another border ½" more toward the outside. You will have two rectangles drawn, one 3" from the edge and another 2½" from the edge. Cover the entire border area, with a strip of ½" masking tape along the inner border and paper to cover the rest.

Using fairly thin blue acrylic paint on an old toothbrush, begin to spatter paint on the inner area. Spatters should be light in the center and heavier toward the edges.

Transfer patterns of trees and stars to acetate or stencil paper and cut out the design with a craft knife. Arrange the stencils as desired (see photograph). Paint the trees and stars with a blunt-tipped stencil brush and acrylic paints. Use your finger dipped in blue paint to make a drift of snow at the base of each tree, rubbing lightly to blend.

When the center design dries, cover it completely with paper. Leave the ½" masking tape in place and paint the outer border red. When the red dries, make random dots of white, green and gold to give a calico effect (dip a sharpened pencil-shaped typing eraser into paint; then pounce up and down to make dots).

Allow the "calico" to dry, expose the inner border by pulling off the tape, and paint it gold. When all paint is dry, give the entire floorcloth at least two coats of varnish.

TREES ON RIBBONS:
pattern on page 129
½ yd. green fabric with small print
green thread
red ribbon (½"-wide)

Cut 10 trees according to pattern. Cut 5 pieces of red ribbon to the correct lengths. (See the photographs for placement of the trees.)

Sew around the outline of each tree with a ¼" seam, catching the end of the ribbon beneath the stitching at the top, and leaving an opening for turning. Clip the seams, turn, and press. Slip stitch the opening closed. Tie a small bow around each ribbon; then attach the decorations to the underside of the mantel or the top of the window frame with masking tape. Hide the tape with boughs of greenery if necessary.

A FOREST OF EVERGREENS

Trees, trees, trees! Plump sculptured trees standing at attention, cheery beribboned trees hanging at the window, and a whole procession of trees encircling the table say in no uncertain terms that Christmas is coming! The bright green fabric of the trees and red satin ribbons are a crisp accent for the white overskirt and deeper green table skirt. An arrangement of juicy apples and tiny candles waiting to be lit on Christmas Eve add even more color to this pleasant setting.

LARGE TABLE SKIRT:

The skirt is simply a large circle of fabric cut to the proper size and hemmed. To find the correct size for your table, measure it carefully; then add the diameter of the top, plus two times the distance from the floor to the top, plus 2″ for hems. The sum is the diameter of the circle you need to cut. (For example, the correct size for a table measuring 30″ wide and 26″ tall would be 30″, plus 26″, plus 26″, plus 2″, for a total of 84″.)

Most table skirts are so large that the fabric must be pieced together to make it wider before the circle is cut. To piece the fabric, cut one length slightly longer than the maximum you need; then add one more length on each side (this may be made from a single length split down the middle). Press the seams open and treat as one piece of fabric.

Fold the fabric into fourths—end to end, then side to side. Tie a string around a pencil and pin the end of the string at the center corner where the folds meet; the distance between the pin and the pencil should equal half the diameter of the circle you are cutting. Holding the pencil upright, draw an arc on the top layer of fabric. Double check your measurements with a yardstick before cutting. Cut through one layer at a time, using the first cut as your guide for cutting the other layers. Unfold the fabric and you will have a circle. Turn under the edge ½″, press, turn under again ½″, press again, and machine stitch to form the hem.

TABLE OVERSKIRT:
patterns on pages 128 and 129
1½ yds. (54″-wide) white fabric
1 yd. green fabric with small print
green thread
6 yds. (½″-wide) red satin ribbon

This overskirt, with a finished diameter of 53″, is suitable for use on a table measuring 30″ or less across the top. (The table in the photograph is 30″ across; on a smaller table the cloth would hang lower on the sides.)

Following the instructions given for making the large table skirt, cut a circle of white fabric that is 54″ in diameter. From the green fabric, cut 12 trees and 12 scallops. Sew the scallops together at the side seams, with right sides together, to form a circle of scallops. Press the seams open.

Place the right side of the ring of scallops on the wrong side of the circle of white, with the outer edges of both together. Pin in place. Sew through both fabrics with a ¼″ seam allowance, following the outside edge of the scallops. Trim excess white fabric so that the edge conforms to the scallops. Clip at intervals around each scallop, especially at the corners, turn, and press.

Turn under ¼″ at the top edge of each scallop, clipping the curves, and press. Top stitch around the turned-under edge.

Turn under the edges of the trees ¼″, clipping the corners and curves as necessary, and press. Center a tree over each scallop, pinning in place. Topstitch around edges.

Cut the ribbon into 18″ lengths. Tie into bows and tack or pin to each point where scallops are seamed together.

SOFT SCULPTURE TREES:
patterns on page 128 and 129
½ yd. green fabric
green thread
polyester batting
wood scraps
drill with a 5/16″ bit
wooden dowels (5/16″-diameter)
woodworker's glue
green spray paint

Cut as many trees from green fabric as desired, making certain that you cut 2 of the same size for each tree. Place fabric with right sides together and stitch around the outlines of each with a ¼″ seam, leaving the bottom open for turning. Clip curves, turn, and press. Stuff with polyester batting.

Cut as many bases as you need from wood; the bases should be at least 3″ square. Drill a hole into the center of each base. Cut the dowel into various lengths for the stands, then insert one into each base, gluing it in the hole. Spray with green paint and let dry.

Sharpen the dowel end of each stand in a pencil sharpener; then push one into the bottom of each tree. Slip stitch the bottom of the trees closed around the dowel.

SNOWFLAKES & MORE SNOWFLAKES

Shimmering satin snowflakes blanket the skirt of this tree—adding a touch of wintry beauty to indoor decorations. Matching gift wrap and satin ornaments create such a spectacular effect that it's hard to believe how simple it is to make them. The secret? Snowflake stencils cut from paper, and several cans of metallic spray paint! Even a kindergarten child can help by cutting some of the snowflakes.

YOU WILL NEED:
notebook or typing paper
spray paint (several shades of metallic colors, available at most hobby or auto supply stores)

artist's spray adhesive for mounting paper
1⅓ yds. (45″-wide) white satin fabric—for tree skirt
1⅓ yds. (45″-wide) lining fabric—for tree skirt
6½ yds. wide double-fold bias seam-binding—for tree skirt
fusible interfacing—for ornaments
extra yardage of satin—for more ornaments (optional)
solid white tissue paper or gift wrap
gold thread

SNOWFLAKES: Fold paper according to the diagram. Use sharp scissors to cut folded paper into various shapes, making some snowflakes large and some small. The more variety you have, the more beautiful the skirt will be. The snowflakes may be reused many times, so you won't need more than 15 or 20—unless you are having too much fun to stop making them.

TREE SKIRT: Basically, the skirt is nothing more than a lined circle of satin with the raw edges bound by bias tape. To make the skirt, fold 1⅓ yds. of satin fabric so that it is in four equal parts. (Fold it end to end, then side to side.) Locate the corner where the folds meet at the center of the fabric. Tie a pencil onto one end of a string long enough to reach from this center corner to the side edge. Hold the string down tightly at the corner with your finger, and draw an arc on the fabric. Cut along this penciled line, then through each successive layer of fabric, using the first cut as your guide. When the fabric is unfolded, it will be a perfect circle. Repeat the process to cut a lining exactly the same size. Set the lining aside.

Cover the floor with newspapers and spread the satin circle flat, shiny side up. Spray the back of each paper snowflake with a coat of artist's adhesive. Position the snowflakes as desired, pressing them firmly onto the satin with your hands. Shake the spray paint well, and spray a very light coat from directly above. Pull up the paper to reveal a reverse-stenciled snowflake on the satin. Work around the skirt, using the same snowflakes over and over, until the whole piece has been sprayed. Even the sprayed areas will retain the satiny look.

Place the satin over the lining, wrong sides together, and pin. Sew around edges ¼" from edge. Make a straight cut toward center on one side, and cut a hole approximately 5" in diameter in the middle. Bind the raw edges with double-fold bias tape.

ORNAMENTS: Use the scraps of satin left from the skirt for the ornaments, or make more from additional yardage. Make a sandwich of two layers of satin placed with wrong sides together and a layer of fusible interfacing between. Press to join all layers. Cut into circles of various sizes. Place adhesive

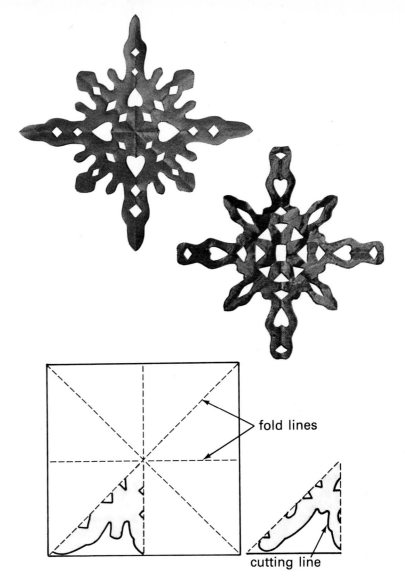

fold lines

cutting line

sprayed snowflake on one side, pressing it down with your fingers, and lightly spray with paint. Peel off snowflake and repeat for other side. Glue a loop of gold thread at the top for hanging. The paper snowflakes themselves may also be hung on the tree when you have finished using them as stencils.

GIFT WRAP: Use the "press and spray" technique described above on solid white tissue paper or gift wrap. Create interesting effects by making short sweeps and spatters of several different colors of paint on the same piece of paper. Harmonizing gift wrap may be spattered with the same paints, but without the snowflake stencils. Set aside each piece after spraying and allow to dry.

HAVE FUN WITH BOWS

There are a dozen ways to add a little unexpected fun to holiday decorations with these snappy ribbon bows attached to clothespins. Clip one onto the tree, use one in place of a napkin ring, or even hold back the curtains in true Christmas style. Pop one on a package, fancy up Fido's collar, or plant one on a poinsettia pot before giving it to a friend.

YOU WILL NEED (to make one bow):
spring-type clothespin
green spray paint
48" (⅞"-wide) non-woven-edge ribbon
thin floral wire
hot glue
small cones (alder or hemlock), statice,
   licopodium, acorns

Spray the clothespin with green paint. Make a bow by looping the ribbon and holding it with a short piece of floral wire twisted around the center. Fluff out the loops of the bow before attaching it to the top of the clothespin with hot glue. Glue on a trimming of natural cones or acorns surrounded by statice and licopodium.

 FELIZ NAVIDAD!

Celebrate the season with a joyously colorful centerpiece of birds wheeling in flight
above a nest of green. Tasseled napkin rings,
curly-topped candleholders, and striped table
runners add to the lively South-of-the-Border
theme.

Aluminum soft drink cans are "recycled"
to make both the birds and candleholders—
the pliable metal is an excellent (and free!)
craft material that is thin enough to cut with
ordinary kitchen shears or scissors. Make
enough birds so that you can hang them in
the tree as ornaments or place some in
plants around the room.

BIRDS:
pattern on page 124
aluminum soft drink cans
shiny enamel paints in bright colors
household cement
drinking straws (paper or plastic)
green plastic foam ring

It takes one regular-sized soft drink can to
make each bird. Cut away the top and rim
of the can; then cut down the length, and
remove the bottom to form a rectangular
piece of aluminum. Place the pattern over
the metal and trace the outlines with pencil

to leave an impression. Cut the body and wings, flattening the body if necessary. Paint both sides of each piece and add details in a contrasting color after the base coat dries.

Bend the wings in the center and glue with household cement to the upper edge of the body. If you have trouble making the wings stay in place, staple once to hold them and hide the staple with paint.

Cut drinking straws to various lengths and paint to match the birds. Slit the top of each straw to hold the bird in place. Insert sprigs of evergreens in the ring of plastic foam; then arrange the birds around the ring to look as though they are flying. Trim with cones if desired.

RUNNERS AND NAPKIN RINGS:

Cut lengths of striped fabric (18"-wide) to hang over the sides of the table about 9". Turn under all edges twice and sew with a zigzag stitch. For napkin rings, wrap rings of heavy paper with yarn; trim with tassels on another length of yarn.

CANDLEHOLDERS:
aluminum soft drink cans
shiny enamel paints in bright colors
needle-nosed pliers
household cement

Each candleholder is made from one small-sized soft drink can and half of a regular-sized can glued together. To make the curly top, first cut away the top of one can, including the rim. Using kitchen shears, cut straight down to make ¼"-wide strips. (This will make a "fringe" around the top of the can.) Paint the cut can both inside and out with the base coat *before* you curl it.

Wrap each strip around the end of the pliers, bending and curling the strips in a symmetrical pattern. Designs will vary greatly depending on how far down you cut and whether you curl each strip or alternate ones. Glue each curled top to a painted can turned upside down. When glue dries, paint on details with contrasting colors.

TORTILLAS OLÉ!

Here is a most unconventional way to use that nourishing staple of Mexican cooking, the tortilla—as part of a Christmas arrangement! Corn tortillas, cut to resemble flowers, are glued to wire stems and allowed to dry naturally. The resulting blossoms, with their gently curved petals and centers of brown, are lovely in combination with greenery and are almost guaranteed to stimulate conversation among your friends.

YOU WILL NEED:
corn tortillas (fresh or frozen)
floral wire (18 gauge)
brown floral tape
silicon glue
plastic spray

If tortillas are frozen, thaw before using. Cut each tortilla into the shape of a flower with 6 to 8 petals, using kitchen shears or a sharp knife. Cut floral wire to the length you desire for the stem, and bend one end to form a small loop. Cover the loop by wrapping it with brown floral tape—this will be the stamen. Poke the other end of the stem through a hole in the center of the flower so that the loop remains on top.

Turn the flower upside down, anchoring the loop in plastic foam or otherwise holding it in place. Apply enough silicon glue at the base to hold the flower and stem firmly together. Allow to dry upside down. The petals will curve as they dry to form a more natural shape. The finished flowers are brittle and are apt to break easily—spray them with a coat of clear plastic to strengthen them, if desired. Arrange the tortilla flowers in a container with greenery, dried chili peppers, and evergreen cones.

Miniature ears of corn, trimmed with wild wheat and strawflowers, form a glowing sunburst to hang on the tree. Attach the corn to a circle of hardboard with hot glue and add a sturdy wire hanger.

CHRISTMAS IN THE SOUTHWEST

Christmas decorations vary widely in different parts of the country because of the diverse plant materials native to each area. Here, the bounty of the great Southwest is displayed to perfection in a garland draped at the window to catch the December sunlight. The earth tones of dried artichokes, gourds, and grasses, and the more vibrant colors of corn and chili peppers are a rich complement to their surroundings.

Create a similar garland by making small bunches of various natural materials. Wrap a short length of cotton twine around each one and knot before tying the bunches to a longer piece of heavier twine which serves as the base. Continue adding materials until the garland is thick and full.

STARLIGHT STARBRIGHT

A million stars dance and twinkle on an indoor tree—adding nighttime magic to holiday parties. Attach strings of miniature white lights with dark green cords to the branches of a ficus tree or other large indoor plant, just as you would to a Christmas tree. The lights may be left on the plant permanently with no harmful results. They are almost invisible during the day but will bathe the room in starlight each evening.

Heap a crystal punchbowl with richly gleaming satin balls—then dim the lights and delight your guests. Wind a string of tiny white bulbs among the multi-colored balls; the cord can be almost hidden from sight as it hangs over the back of the bowl.

Complete the festive decorations by putting a temporary cover on your usual accent pillow. Colorful felt ornaments, trimmed with glittery gold, are appliquéd to the cover with see-through nylon thread.

HOLIDAY PILLOW COVER:
patterns on page 125
fabric to cover pillow front and back
felt scraps in bright colors
gold rickrack, braid, and beads
1½ yds. narrow gold braid
transparent nylon thread for sewing

Add 1¼" to both the length and width of your own pillow; cut 2 pieces of fabric to these measurements and set aside. Cut pattern pieces from felt. Use zigzag stitch to sew felt pieces together. Stitch on gold braid and rickrack; then add beads by hand.

Cut 3 pieces of narrow braid. Pin to pillow front extending from top edge to point where they will meet ornaments. Tie a gold bow around each; then zigzag down the length, catching bow. Pin appliqués in place, overlapping ends of braid. Zigzag around edges. Stitch front and back together with a ⅝" seam, leaving opening at bottom. Insert pillow; slipstitch opening closed.

17

A GOLDEN FANTASY

All that glitters is not real gold, but these gleaming decorations add the Midas touch to any room. The effect of so much gold is dazzling, to say the least, but if ever there is a time to indulge in fantasy, it is during the Christmas season. Fans over the fireplace, dozens of ornaments trailing ribbon streamers, and miles of metallic garlands heighten the lavish effect.

MANTEL FANS—Crisply pleated fans made from foil gift wrap add a bit of glamour to the arrangement of glossy green leaves with gold glass balls. Despite its showy appearance, this mantel decoration costs very little, since the fans require only a single jumbo roll of paper.

To make the large fan, cut a length of gift wrap twice as long as the width of the paper. (If the paper is 26" wide, cut the piece 52" long.) Fold lengthwise down the middle so that the foil shows on both sides. Pleat with 1"-wide folds, stapling once at the bottom to hold the fan in shape. Make the smaller fans in the same way, but cut the paper so that its length equals its width.

FAN ORNAMENTS—Two types of ornaments are shown. One is a miniature version of the fans for the mantel. Instead of stapling fans together, punch a hole through all folds and knot with ribbon streamers.

The punched fans are made from clear acetate covered with a thin sheet of adhesive-backed gold-toned Mylar®. Press the two sheets of plastic together before cutting into a fan shape. (See pattern on page 124.) Place the fan over a thick layer of folded newspapers and use a hat pin or awl to punch little holes through the back of both layers in a freeform design. Tiny pinpoints of light will show through these punched holes as they hang on the tree. At the bottom of the fan, make two larger holes with a hole-punch. Thread these with several 15"-long gold ribbon streamers.

GARLAND—The golden tones of this foil garland come from an unusual source—the foil paper used to wrap baked potatoes in restaurants. (Purchase it at restaurant supply stores.) Aluminum foil may be substituted if you prefer a silvery effect. Cut the foil into 3" squares and crush into small balls by rolling between your gloved hands. Thread the balls into a rope with nylon fishline.

BRAZILIAN STITCHERY

Embroidery, raised to a high degree of skill, is featured on these lovely ornaments. The technique, commonly referred to as Brazilian embroidery, uses rayon flosses in raised stitches to give a three-dimensional effect. The intricacy comes from the fact that a number of different stitches are combined and a number of colors used.

Each ornament uses one panel of three floral designs. The three fabric panels are embroidered over diamond-shaped bases of stiff paper and are then sewn together. A silken tassel completes this exotic ornament.

The lustrous beauty of the stitching depends on the proper choice of flosses. Use any of the following types: EDMAR "Lola," "Frost," or "Brazilian"; MARLITT; J. & P. COATS "Strandsheen." Choose any combination of thread types or colors for a variety of effects. See page 123 for instructions in making individual stitches.

YOU WILL NEED (to make one ornament):
pattern on page 124
9" x 6" opaque silk or polyester fabric
9" x 6" file-folder-weight paper
stick glue
rayon embroidery floss (described above)
#3 or #5 millinery needles
regular embroidery needles

Cut three pattern shapes from file-folder paper. Cut three pieces of fabric; note that the fabric pieces are slightly larger than the paper pieces so that fabric will wrap around edges marked "A" and "B." Rub the right side of each paper tab with the glue stick and press onto the wrong sides of the cut fabric pieces. Rub the glue stick on the underside of edges marked "A" and "B"; turn under fabric along these edges and press to stick in place.

Pencil the design on each fabric piece. (See designs on next page.) Draw a circle (¼"-diameter) for large flowers, and a smaller circle for each bud. The circle serves as a guide when you embroider the first row of petals. Mark only those leaves to be worked in fishbone stitch.

Rayon floss (described above) is used throughout in making these ornaments. Before threading the needle, the floss *must* be straightened by wiping it with a damp cloth and letting it dry before knotting.

When working the embroidery on each panel, begin with the large flowers, then work the buds, and finally the stems and leaves. Use the following procedure when doing all petals on both buttonhole flower and bullion poppy: Come UP (1) through both paper and fabric, then DOWN (2) and UP (3) with needle through fabric only. Either wrap thread around the needle, or cast on threads; then go back DOWN (4) through both fabric and paper. Sew through both fabric and paper at the beginning and ending of all other flowers, buds, stems and fishbone-stitch leaves.

Complete the embroidery on all three panels of the ornament; then fold and pin together. Sew the edges of the fabric together with matching thread, using blind stitch. Embroider along edges with coral knot stitch. Leave a loop of floss at the top for hanging.

Make a tassel from 20 or 25 (6"-long) pieces of different colored flosses, tied together at center with a long strand of floss (to be used later to attach tassel to ornament). Fold flosses end to end; wrap other lengths of floss around the top in one or two places, pulling tightly to hold and tucking ends inside the tassel. Sew on tassel.

LAZY DAISY: Work flower and buds in an elongated lazy daisy stitch with a bullion knot (using 4 wraps) at the end of each petal. Work center of flower in satin stitch with outline stitch around the edge. Work leaves in fishbone stitch and stems in long running stitches (couched if necessary).

BUTTONHOLE FLOWER: Draw a circle (¼"-diameter) for center of large flower and smaller circles for buds. Draw on remaining parts of design very lightly if at all. Use a #3 or #5 millinery needle with a single strand of floss. Beginning at the center, follow steps 1 through 4 given as basic procedure, casting on 12 threads before finishing petal. Overlap the end of the first petal slightly with the beginning of the second, and so on—always working outwards. As you work around the circle, add more cast-on stitches on each row, until you are casting on about 25 threads for each petal. This will increase the size of the petals and cause them to curve. Make 2 French knots for center of large flower.

To make buds, use same floss as for flower, casting on from 8 to 12 threads. For stems, use one strand of floss in outline stitch. For leaves, use one strand and lazy daisy stitch.

BULLION POPPY: Use a #3 or #5 millinery needle. Work flowers in bullion knot petals, working first row around a ¼" circle. On this first row of overlapping petals, use 20 wraps. Make a second row, using 30 wraps for each petal, and a third row, using 40. Work buds with 8 to 10 wraps and make a French knot in center of each. Work stems in back stitch and leaves in lazy daisy stitch.

LAZY DAISY WITH BULLION KNOT

BUTTONHOLE FLOWER

BULLION POPPY

A FRIENDLY WELCOME

There is no plant more symbolic of peace and plenty than corn. Grown in fields all across America, the corn plant is used for food throughout the year and as decoration during the fall and winter months. A wreath of unpretentious cornhusks instantly conveys a message of genuine "Welcome," whether it is on the door of a fine house or a cabin in the woods.

YOU WILL NEED:
cornhusks
straw wreath form
    (15" diameter)
wire floral pins
wire for hanging

Many craft stores sell cornhusks which have been dried and pressed flat. Another obvious way to get husks, of course, is to buy full ears at the grocery store, eat the corn for dinner, and collect the inner husks. If the husks are saved in mesh bags where air can circulate, they will dry in a few days. Should they become mottled or mildewed, bleach the husks for about 30 minutes in a large bowl of water to which you have added ¼ cup of liquid bleach. Rinse well.

Trim each husk to approximately 8" x 2" and thoroughly saturate with water before using. (If husks are shaped when wet, they retain the shape permanently after they dry.) Bend a strip of husk into a loop and attach to the inner rim of the straw wreath form with a wire floral pin, catching both ends of the loop. (See diagram.) Continue adding loops, working around the form in a single row and overlapping the preceding loop by about 2". Complete the first row before beginning the second.

Follow the same process on the second row, but turn the loops in the opposite direction. Continue adding rows of loops, alternating the direction until the wreath form is completely covered. Attach a wire loop for hanging to the back of the wreath. Add trimmings if desired.

GREENERY CLUSTER

If you enjoy arranging natural greenery, consider making a luxuriant foliage cluster instead of a wreath for your door this year. By varying the greenery or the size, the cluster may be scaled to suit almost any style of architecture, whether traditional or contemporary. The expense is minimal, as you probably have a wealth of plant materials nearby for clipping.

YOU WILL NEED:
green plastic foam (approximately 6" x 10")
floral wire (medium gauge)
wire coat hanger
greenery pins (or heavy wire bent into a
    V-shape)
assorted evergreen clippings (magnolia,
    pine, boxwood, cedar, holly, etc.)
bow (optional)
small kitchen sponge (optional)

Cut the greenery with longer stems than you think you will actually need—this gives you more freedom in arranging them and allows you to follow the natural lines of the branches. Stand the branches in a bucket of water for several hours to let them absorb as much moisture as possible. Bend the wire coat hanger and tie it tightly to the plastic foam base with floral wire. Hold the coat hanger in place with greenery pins.

Begin by inserting the longest pieces of greenery into the base, forming a vertical line. Then add shorter pieces of foliage to fill in the rest of the shape, completely covering the base. Place a big bow in the center of the cluster, if desired, holding it with pins. Protect the door by attaching a kitchen sponge to the back of the base.

 COOKIE TREE

Just imagine having a whole Christmas tree decorated with delicious cookies. It's tempting enough to bring out the child in almost anyone. And when the adult realizes that, except for the lights, all of the trimmings cost only about $6.00—then the tree seems even more special!

Most of the cookies on the tree are purchased and used just as they come from the box, but there are a few homemade sugar cookies, beautifully decorated with Royal Icing. (See recipes on pages 95 and 97.) Each cookie hangs from a snippet of bright red yarn.

To add holes to purchased cookies, heat a few at a time in a 300° oven for about two minutes. Punch with a plastic drinking straw well inside the edge so that the cookie's own weight won't break it at the hole. Work quickly, before the cookies have time to cool. If the straw won't punch through, the cookie probably isn't warm enough—put it back into the oven. To add holes to homemade cookies, punch with a drinking straw either before baking or just after the cookies come from the oven.

A delightful tree topper can be made from sugar cookie dough, rolled to about a 3/8" thickness. Cut out the dough in the shape of a star, and, working on a cookie sheet, press the star onto a 12"-long (3/16"-diameter) dowel. Bake the cookie, dowel and all, in a 350° oven until lightly browned. Cool completely before lifting from the cookie sheet. The star may be left plain or decorated with icing. Wire the dowel to the top branch of the tree, and tie with a ribbon or clip on a pert clothespin bow. (See page 10 for the instructions.)

Complete the theme by using extra cookies as package tie-ons. Children will love being able to eat some of their gift wrapping.

A CHRISTMAS VILLAGE

Little eyes will gaze with delight at this tiny Christmas village lined up on a mantel or table. Don't be surprised if some of the houses seem to be rearranged after a while—these houses are so much like blocks that children just can't resist playing with them. The warm colors and hand-painted architectural details on the houses may be varied to suit your own taste and decor. How about changing this Victorian village to a rip-roaring Western town or to a neighborhood of storefronts?

YOU WILL NEED:
4 feet (2″ x 4″) lumber
table saw or circular saw
small handsaw
sandpaper
acrylic paints

Construct this tiny town from stock 2″ x 4″ lumber. A piece 4′ long will be enough to make from 20 to 30 houses.

Set a table saw or circular saw to make cuts at a 45° angle. Rip the entire length of the lumber twice, cutting off corners at 45° to form a roofline (see diagram).

Reset the saw for a 90° cut; then saw the 2″ x 4″ in half to make two 2′-long pieces. Cut a 1″-thick piece from the base of one of these (see diagram). This will make a group of shorter houses. Rip the long narrow piece you have just cut down to ½″ x ½″. This will be used to make the chimneys.

Cut each length of 2″ x 4″ wood into pieces ranging from ¾″- to 3″-wide to make houses of different widths. Use a handsaw to cut the ½″ x ½″ piece into chimneys of various heights, alternating 45° and 90° cuts. Glue chimneys to roofs.

Sand all edges well. Dilute acrylic paints with a little water, and brush onto houses and chimneys for a stained effect. Use a small artist's brush to add details such as doors and windows.

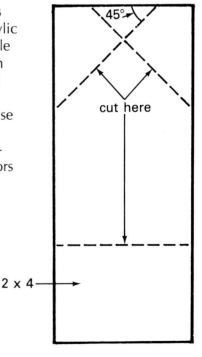

 NATURAL BEAUTIES

Take a moment to marvel at a pine cone. The intricate whorls at its base and its delicate petals resembling those on a flower almost seem to contradict the fact that a pine cone is one of nature's sturdiest vehicles for carrying seeds.

Display the beauty of pine cones on your door this season. The basic wreath has large cones in subtle colors accented by bits of red and green. The other has a trimming of showy "hibiscus" blossoms made from the dried stems of split-leaf philodendrons.

BASIC PINE CONE WREATH:
wire wreath form
pine cones in various sizes and shapes
floral wire (#20 gauge)
trimmings (optional)

Use dry and fully opened cones to make the wreath. Wrap an 8"-length of floral wire around the base of each cone so that it is hidden within the petals. Twist the ends of the wire together, leaving at least one end long enough to attach to the wire form. Join smaller cones into bunches. After cones are wired, soak them in water for a few minutes—they will close up tightly.

Begin with larger cones, adding smaller ones to fill up the remaining spaces. Attach each cone by twisting the floral wire at its base around the wire of the wreath form. After completing the wiring, place the wreath where it can dry naturally. As they dry, the cones will open, making a tighter and fuller wreath. Trim with holly sprigs, lacquered cherries, or other additions.

26

HIBISCUS WREATH:
12"-diameter wire wreath form
medium-gauge covered tying wire
25-30 white pine cones
60-100 spruce pine cones
25 or more Scotch pine cones
3 "hibiscus" flowers (described below)
clear plastic spray

There is an amazing variety of cones available; if you are unable to find the specific kinds mentioned, substitute any others.

Wedge the white pine cones firmly into a tight circle around the wreath form, with their petals over the wires to hold them in place. Wire 4 to 6 spruce pine cones into a bunch; then fasten enough of these bunches along the inside edge of the wreath to cover the flat ends of the white pine cones. Fill in to cover the outer wires of the wreath form with Scotch pine cones, wiring these in place. Add a spray made from 3 "hibiscus" flowers as a trimming. Coat the entire wreath with clear plastic spray.

"HIBISCUS" FLOWER:
5 dried spathes split-leaf philodendron
1 stamen made from a vertical seed pod,
  the center cob of a pine cone, or a
  4"-long cinnamon stick
10" (#20 gauge) floral wire
5" (#16 gauge) floral wire
brown floral tape

When a leaf from a large split-leaf philodendron (Selloum) dies, the stem and the portion that forms its base dry up and are easily detached from the plant. This wide base, called a spathe, provides a strong and flexible material to use in many crafts.

Cut five 5"-long pieces from the spathes. Soak overnight; then stretch out fibers with your fingers to form petals. Thread a 10"-long wire through all 5 petals about 1" from the end. Trim away square edges.

Prepare stamen by taping it to a 5" length of heavy wire. Draw petals into a circle by pulling ends of wire together with pliers. Insert stamen; then cover all exposed wire, as well as base of petals, with floral tape. Shape petals into a natural-looking flower while damp, holding in position with clothespins. Let flowers stand until dry.

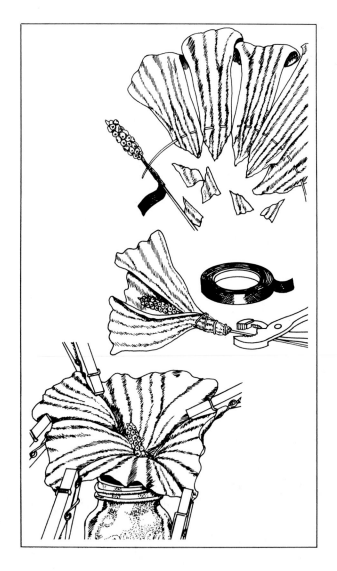

PARTY TIME

Your friends won't believe what they're seeing—a wreath made entirely from crackers! Hang it on the wall over a table spread with snacks and listen to the admiring comments from your guests.

YOU WILL NEED:
2 rings cut from corrugated cardboard
crackers (5 or 6 kinds—light and dark)
hot glue or quick-setting cement
glossy spray varnish
wire loop for hanging

Use a craft knife to cut two rings from heavy cardboard. The larger one should be approximately 12" across with a 6"-wide hole in the center, while the smaller one should be 10" across with an 8"-wide hole. Glue the two wreath forms together, spacing them with a stack of 1"-square pieces of cardboard in several places.

Pour each kind of cracker you are using into a separate bowl. Begin with largest crackers, and end with the smallest, keeping the wreath completely flat as you work. Glue a row of crackers around the outer edge of the large ring, overlapping the cardboard. Repeat with another row of crackers around the inner rim. Continue adding crackers to cover bare spots, each time going around the wreath so that it will be symmetrical.

When all gaps are covered, you may wish to add cracker "poinsettias" such as those shown in the photograph. Choose a pointed cracker for these, clustering several together on end to form the petals. The leaves and center are made from still another type of pointed cracker. Glue on a wire loop.

Spray several light coats of varnish on both front and back sides of wreath, handling very carefully to avoid breaking the crackers. If one should accidentally break, scrape away any piece remaining, glue another in its place, and varnish. The wreath should easily last throughout the entire season, but the fragile nature of the crackers will eventually cause it to crumble.

 ## GINKGO FLOWERS

Who would believe that these graceful golden-beige flowers are made of fallen leaves? The fan-shaped leaves of the ginkgo (or maidenhair) tree are wired together on stems to form blossoms that look amazingly similar to double peonies. Arranged in a container or trimming a wreath, the flowers are a lovely embellishment of nature's art.

Gather the leaves in the fall as soon as they drop from the tree, before wind and weather mar their fragile structure. The ripple-edged leaves with their delicate veining have the appearance of antique parchment but a very light coating of plastic spray gives a waxy luster to the finished flowers.

YOU WILL NEED:
ginkgo leaves
brown floral tape
floral wire (#18 gauge)
clear plastic spray

Select a large ginkgo leaf and roll it into a tight coil to form the center. Tightly wrap floral tape around the center, catching both the base and the stem. Do not break the tape, but continue adding leaves with one hand and wrapping with the other, until the flower is the desired fullness. Add a wire stem and wrap with tape until completely covered. Coat lightly with clear plastic spray.

CHRISTMAS CARDINALS

Drape a staircase with garlands of greenery, and trim it with a flock of cardinals so real they'd almost fool a cat! Glossy red paper forms the body of each bird, while the wings and tail are made with crisply pleated tissue paper. A few of these cardinals perched on houseplants around the room will add a happy surprise to your Christmas decorating.

YOU WILL NEED:
pattern on page 125
heavy red paper (preferably with a
   glossy coating)
black marking pen
red tissue paper
stapler
white household glue

The paper must be red on both sides; if you are unable to find double-sided paper, glue two pieces together.

Transfer the pattern of the body to waxed paper or tracing paper. Draw over the lines again with a dull pencil to leave an impression on the heavy red paper beneath. (Carbon paper may also be used to transfer the pattern.) Cut around this indented line to make the body of the bird. Using the pattern as a guide, draw the beak and the eye with a black marking pen.

Cut one wing (6" x 4½") and one tail (5½" x 2½") from red tissue paper. Fold each piece accordion-style on the shorter side, making the pleats very narrow.

Hold the pleated tail in place on the body of the bird. Lift the outer pleat on each side and staple through the other pleats and the body. Fold the outer pleats to conceal the staple.

Cut a slit in the body as indicated on the pattern; then slide the pleated wing through the slit so that half sticks out on each side. Pull the back edge of each wing to meet the body and attach with a tiny dot of glue, holding the wing in place with a paper clip until it dries. Spread the wings if necessary.

For each powder puff, make one daisy from white yarn, following directions on the Daisy Loom package. Glue the powder puff to the center of the daisy.

Cut face and cap from felt scraps. Glue the pieces to the powder puff, using the photograph as a guide. Fold down the point of the cap, secure with glue, and add ball fringe. Attach a cord for hanging.

DOLLS ON A WREATH

Bright is the word for this unashamedly red and green yarn wreath. Worked in simple crochet stitches, the basic wreath is lined and has a filling of polyester stuffing to make it plump. Fat red yarn and a pair of cheerful yarn dolls add the finishing touches. Hang the wreath inside on a door or window, or even on the front of a cabinet.

YOU WILL NEED:
plastic lid from 2-pound margarine container
craft knife
1 skein each red and green yarn (4-ply worsted weight)
size G crochet hook
½ yd. green polyester knit fabric
polyester stuffing
tapestry needle
jumbo red yarn used for gift ties
small amount blue and yellow 4-ply yarn
black felt scraps

BASIC WREATH—Make a flexible plastic ring by cutting the center from the lid with a craft knife, leaving just the rim. Tie the end of the green yarn to the ring; then sc evenly around the ring, making sure that it is well-covered. Join with sl st.

Row 1: Ch 3 * 3 tr in first sc, sk 1 sc, 3 tr in next sc, repeat from *, join with sl st into top of ch 3. *Row 2:* Ch 3, tr into each tr around, join with sl st into top of ch 3. *Rows 3 through 6:* repeat row 2. Break off yarn, leaving a 45" strand.

SANTA & HIS FRIENDLY ELF

Even someone who doesn't sew a stitch can whip up this jolly Santa and his friendly Elf. Scraps of felt and white yarn trimmings add details to faces made of a most unlikely craft material—plush pink powder puffs. Older children will especially enjoy making these ornaments and can vary the colors and features to create a variety of characters.

YOU WILL NEED:
white 4-ply yarn
Daisy Loom (may be purchased at many craft or needlework shops)
pink velour powder puffs (2¾"-diameter)
felt scraps
ball fringe
white household glue
cord for hanging

Using polyester fabric the color of the green yarn, cut 2 rings the same size that the finished wreath will be. Place right sides together and stitch around both edges; then cut through to the center, turn and stuff with polyester filling. Slip stitch the opening closed. Place the stuffed fabric ring between the double thickness of crocheted yarn.

Thread the loose 45″ strand of yarn into a tapestry needle. Fold the last 3 rows of crochet backwards over the stuffed form and whip the top edge to the back of the ring. Weave the end of the yarn into the back. *Row 7:* Sc evenly around outer edge (between Row 3 and Row 4), sl st into first sc. *Row 8:* Shell st around (*5 dc in next sc, skip next sc, sl st in next sc, repeat from *), break yarn and weave end into back. To make the border, sc with red yarn around edge of shell stitches (see photograph), break yarn, and weave into back.

Thread 3 lengths of jumbo red yarn around the top of the wreath, going over and under the crocheted yarn to make an interesting pattern (see photograph). Tie and cut off the yarn, hiding the ends with yarn dolls.

YARN DOLLS—To make the body of each doll, wrap red yarn 35 times lengthwise around a 3″ x 5″ card. Tie with a bit of red yarn at one end. Cut through the loops at the other end. To make the arms, wrap more red yarn 13 times around the short side of a 3″ x 5″ card. Slide the loops off the card, tie with bits of yarn about ½″ in from each end, and clip through the yarn to form hands.

Place the arms through the middle of the body. Tie the body with yarn above and below the arms to form a head and waist. For the girl, leave the skirt as is; for the boy, separate the yarn in the middle and tie with yarn to form legs. Make hair for the girl from yellow yarn, braiding it and tying blue yarn bows at each end. For the boy, tie on short lengths of yellow yarn for hair. Add a cap made by crocheting a 3″-long chain, then working one triple crochet in each stitch of the chain. Stitch cap together at the ends. Glue on facial features cut from black felt.

Standard Crochet Abbreviations

ch(s)—chain(s)
sc—single crochet
dc—double crochet
tr—triple crochet
sk—skip
st(s)—stitch(es)
sl st—slip stitch
*—repeat whatever follows * as indicated

TEDDY BEARS' PICNIC

"To eat, or not to eat?" That is the question every child will ask himself about these adorable marshmallow teddy bears. Delightful to play with, or to use as a centerpiece, these little fellows will liven up any Christmas party. (Set the table with wipe-clean vinyl runners, stitched around the edges.)

Each bear is dressed to the hilt with ribbon bows, caps, and other holiday finery. Be sure to remove all trimmings and toothpicks before letting very young children eat the bears.

YOU WILL NEED:
large and small marshmallows
granulated brown sugar
waxed paper
toothpicks
chocolate icing for face
hot cinnamon candies for tongue
cake decorating tube with tiny round tip
bits of ribbon with non-woven edges
red fabric-backed vinyl (for runners)

Each bear will require two large marsh-mallows and six small ones. Dampen the marshmallows in water, roll in sugar until completely coated, and set aside to dry on waxed paper.

Push two toothpicks into the flat top of a large marshmallow; add a head by pushing another marshmallow onto the toothpicks (flat side facing forward). Attach legs, arms, and ears made of small marshmallows, using toothpick halves to hold.

Mix icing from powdered sugar, cocoa, and water, adjusting the amount of sugar and water until icing is a "pastry tube" con-sistency. Pipe two dots of icing for eyes, flat-tening them by pressing with a moistened finger. Pipe a mouth, and press on a tongue of cinnamon candy. Cut bits of ribbon for bows, mufflers, caps, and other adornments.

A BIRTHDAY TREE

Do you have a child whose birthday comes around Christmas? After a lifetime of having the birthday lost amidst other celebrating, your child deserves special recognition. This year, decorate a BIRTHDAY TREE es-pecially for him—and watch his eyes light up! Simply poke small balloons into the tree and then festoon the branches with colorful streamers.

A CHILD'S TOY TREE

When your child says "Mommy, I want a tree of my very own," chances are that you have the makings for it right at hand. This tree is made from branches trimmed from a large Christmas tree that needed shap-ing. A cone of plastic foam forms the base, and the limbs are inserted until the miniature tree is a pleasing shape. Most children have dozens of tiny toys that serve beautifully as colorful ornaments when tied onto the tree with yarn. A giant lollipop wired to the upper-most branch completes this whimsical TOY TREE.

LIVING IVY WREATH

Begin rooting cuttings of ivy early, so that by the time Christmas comes, you'll have this impressive wreath made of living plants. A moss-filled wire ring forms the base of the wreath, and rooted cuttings cling to the moss for support.

As spectacular as it appears when used as a centerpiece, this wreath also does well in moderate climates when hung on a wall or fence outdoors. Keep it up year-round, and decorate it for the holidays.

YOU WILL NEED:
2 wire wreath forms (12" or 14" diameter)
sheet moss
fine wire
rooted ivy

Fill one of the wire wreath forms with sheet moss, packing in as much as you possibly can. Cover with the other wreath form, and use the fine wire to wrap securely. Twist ends of wire together, so that wreath forms are carefully fastened together. Soak the wreath base you have just made in water until the moss is wet. Poke holes in the moss with a pencil, and stick the rooted ivy in the holes. Fill as full of ivy as you like—the thicker you plant the ivy, the more luxuriant the wreath will be.

To use the wreath as a centerpiece, place it on a large tray. Fill the center with fat red candles; add bits of baby's breath or dried flowers if desired. A perky bow can be wired to a florist's pick as the finishing touch. Use the wreath in a spot where it will get some sun, watering it twice each week.

BASKETWEAVE PLACEMATS

Simple strips of folded fabric become sturdy and ever-so-colorful placemats when joined in an "over and under" weave. Because each strip is folded 4 layers thick, the mats take quite a bit of fabric. It is a good idea to purchase remnants of fabric in Christmas colors or in shades to complement your room year round. These washable, no-iron mats are exceptionally durable, though, and should give years of service.

This is an ideal project for friends to work on together—one can cut the fabric while the other irons it into folds. Later, one can weave the strips while the other sews.

YOU WILL NEED (to make one mat):
assorted no-iron fabric remnants (to equal about 1½ yards)
14" x 21" cardboard
masking tape
thread to match fabric for the binding

The folded fabric strips may be ½" wide (as shown in the photograph), 1" wide, or a combination of widths. Following the straight grain of the fabric, cut the strips 4 times wider than their finished width will be. For ½"-wide folds, cut the fabric 2" wide; for 1"-wide folds, cut the fabric 4" wide. Then cut the strips into pieces 1" longer than the finished dimensions of the mat. To make a mat that is 12" x 18", you will need enough 19"-long strips for their combined folded widths to equal 12". You will also need enough 13"-long strips for their combined folded widths to equal 18".

Fold the fabric strips so that the raw edges meet in the center; then press. Fold side to side to completely enclose the raw edges, and press again.

Fasten all but two of the 19"-long folded strips to the cardboard with masking tape—the strips should be positioned with their edges just touching each other. Weave the shorter 13"-long strips over and under the longer ones, reserving two strips. Use tape about ½" from the edges to hold in place.

Trim the ends of the strips so that they protrude ⅜" from the edges of the woven portion. Use the reserved strips to bind the outside of the mat, sewing them in place to enclose all raw edges. Remove any tape remaining on the mat.

DOWN THROUGH THE CHIMNEY

Traffic will stop in front of your house at the sight of Santa trying his best to get his plump body down the chimney. Made from sturdy plywood, and painted to look like the jolly old fellow himself, this unusual outdoor decoration is a little larger than life-size. Santa can be used on almost any chimney—each year he is simply re-mounted with bolts into anchors left permanently in place.

A word of caution—use a sturdy ladder when installing Santa. Roofs are often slippery, and chimneys are always high. If your neighbor offers to help with the job, you should let him!

YOU WILL NEED:
patterns on pages 130 and 131
4' x 4' sheet of plywood (½" A.D. exterior grade, preferably fir)
jigsaw with plywood blade
several #8 (1"-long) wood screws
wood filler (if necessary)
exterior wood primer
exterior enamel paints (red, white, black, brown, light brown)
polyurethane varnish
12" (2" x 4") lumber
3 steel angle braces (4" x 4")
3 (2"-long) lag bolts with washers
3 lead anchors to fit lag bolts
drill and bits
wrench to fit lag bolts

Transfer the outlines for both Santa and his bag to the plywood. One 4' x 4' sheet of plywood will be enough for both pieces if you draw Santa's foot separately (see the broken line on the pattern). Cut Santa, the bag, and the foot; then re-join the foot to the leg with a scrap piece of wood attached with screws to the back of both pieces.

Fill in any holes along the edges with wood filler, and sand the filler smooth when it dries. Apply 2 coats of wood primer to all surfaces of each piece, sanding after the last coat. The better you prepare the surface, the

longer Santa will last. Mark the details for painting by making scratched indentations with a nail on the surface of the plywood.

You may wish to trial-fit the pieces before proceeding, marking with an indentation those points where you will need to drill later. Place the straight line of the bag along the side edge of the chimney. Make 2 marks on the bag to show the position of mortar joints near the top and bottom. At the same time, mark those mortar joints so that you can drill them later. Hold Santa's body up to the front of the chimney; the straight line should be even with the top edge. Mark the back of the plywood at two points level with the mortar joints you have just marked. Somewhere on the knee make another mark at a mortar joint.

Paint both Santa's body and the bag with at least 2 coats of enamel, mixing the colors as necessary to get various shades (see photograph). Paint the back of both pieces, as well as the length of 2" x 4", with black enamel. When dry, coat all pieces with clear varnish for the most durable finish.

The 2" x 4" lumber acts as a spacer to separate Santa's body from the bag. Attach the narrow edge of the 2" x 4" to the front of the straight edge of the bag at the two places you have marked, with screws fastened through metal angle braces. (Figure 1.) Place

Figure 1 (viewed from top)

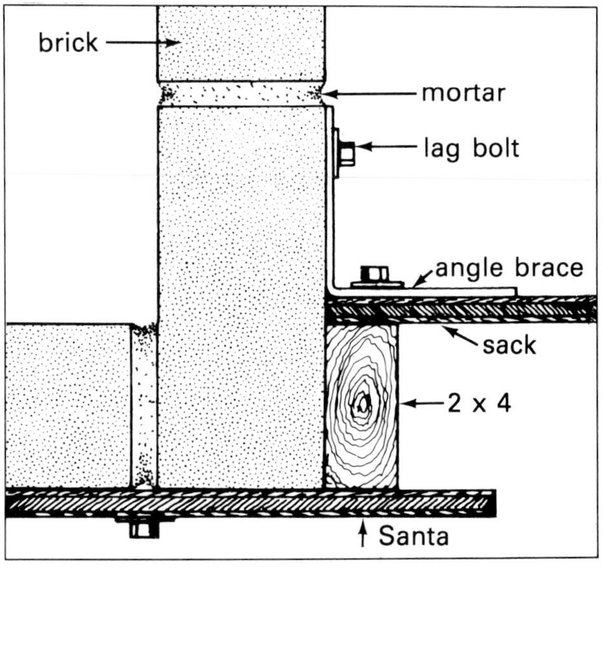

the other narrow edge of the 2" x 4" on the back side of Santa as shown on the pattern, attaching it from the front with a wood screw. Drill a hole in the leg at the point you have marked. Attach another angle brace along the straight edge of Santa's body. (This angle brace will enable you to hang Santa on the chimney as you work.)

Santa is held in place with lag bolts fastened into lead anchors in the mortar joints. (Figure 2.) Hold Santa in place on the chimney; then make pencil marks at three places—one through the hole drilled in the knee, and two more through the holes at the other side of the two metal angles. Drill into the mortar at these points, and hammer the lead anchors into the holes. Fill in any gaps around the anchors with putty.

Hang Santa and his bag on the chimney with the metal angle; then insert the lag bolts into the anchors in the mortar. Tighten the bolts with a wrench so that Santa is held firmly against the chimney. Illuminate Santa with an outdoor spotlight mounted in a tree or elsewhere. This will focus a beam of light on the chimney but not the house.

When you disassemble Santa for storage, keep the lag bolts in the lead anchors to prevent water from accumulating and seeping into the mortar. Store the cut-out in a cool dry place to keep plywood from warping.

Figure 2 (viewed from side)

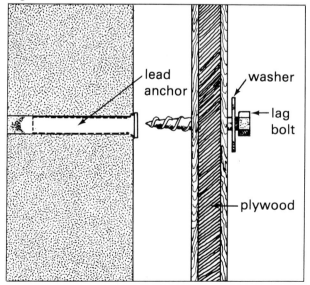

 RED BIRDS IN A WREATH

Fat little baby birds, made from pine cones and nuts, perch on this homey wreath to hang at a kitchen window. The simplicity of twining vines and dried leaves from a dusty miller plant is accented by a bow.

YOU WILL NEED:
dried dusty miller leaves
chestnuts
large and small pine cones
red acrylic paint
vine wreath (8"-diameter)
grosgrain ribbon
white household glue
hot glue or quick-drying cement

Dry dusty miller leaves between paper towels pressed in a flower press or between the pages of a weighted magazine. Press for about three weeks before using.

For each bird, you will need one chestnut, one small pine cone, and 9 petals from a large pine cone. Paint these red, leaving a small unpainted area at the bottom of the chestnut so that glue will stick properly. Dip the bases of 3 pine cone petals into household glue and push into the small cone to form a wing. Repeat for other wing. Form tail with 3 petals and glue. Glue on head with hot glue or quick-drying cement, with pointed end of nut toward front to form a beak. Add eyes with felt-tipped pen.

Tuck dusty miller leaves into the vine wreath until the arrangement is pleasing. Hold each leaf with a dab of household glue. Perch red birds on the wreath, and glue. Add a ribbon loop and bow at the top.

BEAUTIFUL BERRIES

Even if guests are due to arrive at almost any moment, you still have time to create a stunning centerpiece. Loosely arrange cuttings of pine or other evergreens in your most elegant vase, removing any greenery below the water line. Add clusters of berries for color, and tuck an ornament or small holiday accessory beneath the arrangement.

VINE WREATH

Snip a few vines, clip some branches, tie on nuts and berries, and suddenly the natural beauty of the plant material takes on a new artistry. Despite its variety of rich textures, this wreath costs only pennies, making it a good choice for families who are both cost- and style-conscious.

Use grapevines, honeysuckle, or any other long flexible vines to form the base of the wreath. Loop a fairly large vine into a circle of the proper size. Continue looping that vine and others around and through the circle until the wreath is thick and full. No ties are necessary—simply tuck any loose ends into the wreath.

Tie on the evergreen clippings and cones with the thin craft wire that comes on a spool. Drill two holes through the base of each nut, insert a piece of wire through both holes, and twist the ends of the wire before attaching the nut. Several nuts or acorns may be twisted together to form a cluster if desired. After adding the berries to the arrangement, wrap several times with wire to hold them in place.

41

TINY TREASURES

PINE CONE TREES

Select the largest pine cones and the smallest miniatures to make enchanting Christmas trees that are just the right size to tuck in a favorite spot. Whether you cluster them on a table as a centerpiece, or make a special arrangement in the guest room, this is one decoration that you can enjoy for many years. Cushion the trees in a box with tissue paper at the end of the season, and they will be ready to display next year.

Lightly sand the bottom of each miniature. Put a dot of wood glue on a few pine cone petals and on the bottoms of the miniatures,

working with 4 or 5 at a time. Wait for the glue to become tacky; then position the miniatures with tweezers.

CHOIRBOY ORNAMENT

The circular shape of a wooden napkin ring makes a perfect frame for almost anything small enough to be displayed inside. Here, a tiny choirboy opens his mouth in joyful song, but other miniatures would be equally attractive. A bit of gold braid highlights the front of the ring, while a golden cord suspends it from the branch.

VICTORIAN FANCIES

BASKETS WITH SILK FLOWERS

Dainty baskets filled with snowy white blossoms are a lovely reminder that spring follows winter. Import shops or craft supply stores often carry a number of very small baskets, with some being only 2" or 2½" across.

Use any of the wide variety of silk flowers available; perhaps you might echo the colors of poinsettias or cyclamen used elsewhere in your room. Attach the flowers with glue for more permanent ornaments, or arrange loosely so that the baskets may be reused in a different way next year.

LACY FANS

Old-fashioned lacy fans with clusters of ribbon and pastel silk flowers bring romance to the Christmas tree. The delicacy of the white fans against dark green needles makes the ornaments all the more appealing—and the color of the trimmings may vary to suit your decor.

To make fans, cut 12" strips of 4"-wide straight edged lace. Fold gently, accordion-style, without creasing. Wrap thin wire around the base, but allow the top to fan out. Add ribbon bows and tiny silk flowers, holding in place with a dab of white glue.

A WARM & FRAGRANT CORNER

Brighten a dark corner for the holidays by creating a glowing and wonderfully fragrant arrangement of candles, shiny apples sprigged with greenery, and cinnamon-spicy pomanders made from fruits. On the wall above, hang a pungent eucalyptus wreath.

Make the pomanders from firm, unblemished oranges, pears, or lemons, pricking the skin with a nut pick before inserting a whole clove in each hole. Roll the clove-covered fruits in a mixture of equal parts ground cinnamon and powdered orris root (obtained at drugstores). Dry the pomanders for 4 to 6 weeks in a dark drawer or closet.

The drying time may be speeded up by baking them for a few hours in a 200° oven, then continuing to dry them naturally until they are needed. Shake any excess powder from the dried pomanders and decorate with ribbons and other trimmings.

The eucalyptus wreath is made from a base of plastic foam and several bunches of dried eucalyptus. If you are making a 15"-diameter wreath, you may need up to four bunches. Clip each branch of eucalyptus into 4"-5" lengths. Wire three lengths together on a florist's pick to make a full cluster. Insert picks into the base, always working in the same direction, until the base is covered. Twine a ribbon through the wreath and add a bow if desired.

44

CHRISTMAS MORNING STOCKINGS

Do you know a little boy who has all the energy of a bolt of lightning? Or is there a little girl growing up in your home who still likes to plant kisses on your cheek? They're sure to love these lively stockings done in machine appliqué. For background, choose one of the delightful Christmas prints available this time of year, or try a solid fabric with a number of different prints for the appliqué. Both stockings are made the same way; only the fabrics and the designs for the appliqué vary.

YOU WILL NEED:
patterns on pages 132 and 133
½ yd. cotton-blend fabric
½ yd. lining fabric
½ yd. Pellon® fleece or polyester batting
scraps of contrasting prints or solids for appliqué
iron-on interfacing to back appliqués
sewing thread to match your fabrics
3½" narrow ribbon for a hanging loop

Cut a front and back for the stocking from the background fabric. Then, using the same pattern, cut a front and back from the lining fabric, and also from the Pellon® fleece. Set aside these pieces.

Cut the lightning bolt and the star pieces or the hearts from fabric scraps. Cut an equal number of pieces from iron-on interfacing. Press these onto the wrong side of your appliqué fabric, following the ironing instructions given for your particular interfacing. Arrange the now-stiffened cut-outs on the front of the stocking as shown in the photograph or as you desire. Pin in place. Machine appliqué each piece with a zigzag stitch. For best results, first overcast the edges with a narrow, loosely spaced zigzag stitch. Go over this stitching a second time with a slightly wider and more closely spaced outline of zigzag stitching.

Place the front and back pieces with right sides together. Place a corresponding piece of fleece over each one and pin in place. Sew through all 4 layers, ¼" from the edge, using the straight stitch on your sewing machine and leaving the top open. Turn the stocking right side out.

Stitch the lining front and back together, with right sides facing, again with a ¼" seam allowance. Fit the lining into outer stocking, with wrong sides together. Fold in the top edge of each, and pin together. Pin a loop of ribbon at the back, between the two layers. Blind stitch the top edges of outer stocking and lining together, being sure to put extra stitches for strength where the ribbon is attached.

AN ANGEL IN THE WINDOW

Morning sunlight streaming through the brilliant stained glass of this "sun-catcher" will bathe your room in glowing colors as the angel lifts her voice in silent song.

The panel is made using the copper foil method of construction in which each piece of glass is wrapped with copper tape, then joined with solder. The glass design is then encircled with a strip of channel lead, and a chain is added for hanging.

If you prefer to work with glass stains instead of actual stained glass, make a window decoration by this pattern using a round of acrylic, liquid glass stains, and plastic lead that comes from a tube (all available in most craft stores).

YOU WILL NEED:
pattern on page 134
light cardboard
medium point felt-tipped pen
plywood square (for working surface)
glass in your choice of colors
glass cutter
copper foil tape (¼"-wide)
horseshoe nails (for holding glass)
water-based flux
solder (either 60/40 or 50/50)
soldering iron
U-channel lead came (to edge panel)
2" (16-gauge) copper wire
12" brass jack chain (available in most
  hardware stores)
copper sulphate solution (or patina solution made for use with stained glass)
acrylic or oil paints in black and red

Trace pattern and transfer to light cardboard. Cut apart the cardboard pattern, which will be your guide when cutting the glass. Use plywood as a working surface. Place each pattern piece on glass of the proper color, and draw around it with a felt-tipped pen. Cut all individual pieces of glass. After cutting, check to see that pieces fit together correctly by arranging them over the full-size pattern on tracing paper. Correct by recutting if necessary. Small mistakes can be remedied by letting solder fill in gaps.

Wrap the edges of each piece of glass with copper foil tape, pressing down firmly on all sides for better adherence. Place all pieces of foil-wrapped glass in their correct positions over the plywood. Hold glass in place by tacking several sharp-pointed horseshoe nails into the plywood along the perimeter.

Heat soldering iron. Meanwhile, brush all copper tape with flux. Apply dots of solder at all points where corners meet. Once pieces are joined, so that glass holds together, fill in along the rest of the tape by adding more solder. When one side has been soldered, turn the glass over and repeat the entire process on the other side.

Make hair using the same basic "tape and solder" technique. Position short strips of copper tape on the right side of the glass itself, approximating the shape of hair. Cut tiny scallops along the edge of some of the pieces of tape, using these to frame the face like a hairline. Brush copper tape with flux. Drip solder onto the tape, building up a fairly thick layer. The solder will stick to the copper tape, but not the glass. If it is properly applied, the solder will look like ringlets of hair.

Stretch out the channel lead edging and use it to enclose the rough outside of the glass. Join the ends with solder. Attach two rings made from copper wire to the top with solder and add a chain.

Clean the glass thoroughly, first with detergent and then glass cleaner, to remove all traces of flux. For an antique patina, brush the soldered joints with a copper sulphate solution or a patina compound made for use with stained glass. Rinse with water and dry.

Paint facial features with acrylic or oil paints and a tiny brush. Allow to dry. Hang the sun-catcher securely from hooks above the window.

BIRD & BERRIES

This magnificent crewel bird is so realistic you can almost hear him sing. Perched on his wreath of twigs and berries, he deserves a very special spot on your Christmas tree this year. This is not the project for a beginning embroiderer, but if you have mastered your crewel stitches, you should enjoy this opportunity to show off your skill.

YOU WILL NEED:
pattern and color key on page 150
8″ square of cream-colored linen or linen-like fabric
Persian yarns and embroidery flosses (5 yards or less of each)
Fray-Check® (to prevent raveling)
4″-diameter circle of heavy cardboard
4″-diameter circle of polyester batting
4″ circle of white felt
⅔ yard red cord
Have on hand: transfer pencil, tracing paper, white household glue

Using a transfer pencil and tracing paper, trace the outlines of the design and transfer to fabric. Do not cut out at this time. Use a single strand of Persian yarn unless otherwise indicated, and follow the color key.

Work the twig wreath in split stitch with two strands of yarn, using the two colors randomly as shown in the photograph. Outline the twigs in backstitch with one strand of dark brown floss.

Next, work the berries in padded satin stitch. Add a small straight stitch worked with four strands of white floss as a realistic highlight to each berry, using the photograph as a guide.

Work the bird in long-and-short stitch, starting in the facial area and working outward. With a single strand of black floss, work small straight stitches along the feather lines and the outlines of the bird.

Work the eye, beak, and feet in satin stitch with four strands of floss, adding a small white straight stitch for the eye highlight. Outline the beak and the feet in backstitch with a single strand of black floss.

Block the finished embroidery, and cut it into a circle about 5½″ in diameter. Make a ½″-deep clip about every half inch around the outer edge of the circle and apply Fray-Check® to the cut outer edge.

Cut out 4″ circles—one from heavy cardboard, one from white felt, and one from polyester fleece. Place the fleece circle on top of the cardboard circle. Then place the embroidery, right side up, on top. Hold in place and turn over all three layers together. Apply a thin layer of glue to the back edge of the cardboard circle and press down the fabric turnbacks onto the glued edge. Glue the felt circle to the back of the ornament to hide raw edges.

Glue red cord around the outer edge of the ornament, allowing an extra 6″ on each end of the cord to form a loop at the top. About 2″ from the ends, bind the two cords by wrapping them together with a bit of thread or floss. Unravel the cord ends to form a tassel.

CARRY A HOLIDAY PURSE

Resplendent with golden cords and pictures cut from greeting cards, this purse is actually made from a lunchbox. It uses the traditional decoupage technique of many coats of varnish applied with a brush. The time spent on this fairly lengthy process will result in an attractive purse which may be used for many years.

YOU WILL NEED:
metal lunchbox
fine sandpaper
tack rag (obtain from a hardware store)
red enamel paint
gold paint
satin varnish
Christmas cards
gold paper lace or braid (available from
    stores selling decoupage supplies)
white household glue
clear acrylic spray
gold cord or yarn
gold tassel
fabric for lining (velvet, felt, quilted
    fabric, etc.)
thin cardboard

Roughen the outside of the lunchbox by rubbing it with sandpaper; then dust it with a tack rag and apply 2 or 3 coats of enamel. Paint edges, handle, and hinges with gold paint, using a small brush. Apply one coat of varnish over all; avoid letting it run.

Cut favorite motifs from greeting cards, brush the backs with glue, and arrange on the purse. Smooth carefully to eliminate air bubbles. Add gold paper lace if desired. When glue dries, spray with one coat of clear acrylic to set the color in the pictures. (Some dyes run when varnished.)

Apply as many coats of varnish as you wish—the more you use, the more durable the finished purse will be. Allow each coat to dry at least overnight, lightly sand, and

51

dust with a tack rag before applying the next coat. Brush the entire handle with glue, and wrap heavily with gold cord or yarn. Add a tassel if desired.

Cut pieces of cardboard to fit the inside of the purse. These will be covered with fabric and glued in place to make the lining; cut them slightly smaller than the exact measurements. You will need one long piece (bent to go all around the 4 sides), one rectangle cut to fit the bottom, and one rectangle that will curve to fit the inside of the lid.

Spread one side of each piece of cardboard with white glue. Place the cardboard on the wrong side of the fabric and press down. Trim fabric ½" larger than the cardboard on each side; then fold back this allowance and glue to the other side of the cardboard. When all pieces are covered with fabric, spread glue on the back of each piece and press into place. Insert the sides first, then the bottom, and, finally, the lining for the lid.

JINGLE BELL HAIR CLIPS

The cheerful sound of jingle bell hair clips will gladden the heart of any little girl. Make some for your child from bits of ribbon, tiny bells, and small metal curler clips. They are ideal bazaar items, stocking stuffers, or party favors for the younger set.

YOU WILL NEED (to make two clips):
12" (½"-wide) green grosgrain ribbon
12" (½"-wide) red grosgrain ribbon
2 small jingle bells
2 metal curler clips (with pointed ends)
white household glue (optional)

For each clip, form a loop from a 5" piece of green ribbon by stitching ends together or securing with a drop of glue. Make another loop from a 4" piece of red ribbon in the same manner. Flatten the loops and center the red on top of the green, with cut ends down. Wrap 1" of green ribbon around the center of the two loops and glue or stitch ends together on the bottom side. Stitch a jingle bell onto the green ribbon in the center. Finally, stitch or glue the bow to the top of the hair clip. With stitching, there is less chance of the bow coming off.

BARNYARD FRIENDS

Old MacDonald had a farm—and your little boy (or girl) can have one, too. Animal shapes cut from wood will provide hours of fun for would-be farmers around your house. Inside the carrying case, shaped like a barn, are a pig, a horse, a cow, a chicken, and a duck in simple designs painted with bright colors. A child can easily move animals or other toys from room to room.

YOU WILL NEED:
patterns and color key on pages 135-139
1" x 12" x 30" pine shelving
7" x 12¾" (⅛"-thick) hardboard
gloss latex enamel or acrylic paints
woodworking glue
8D finishing nails
12¾" (½"-diameter) wooden dowel
Have on hand: band saw or jigsaw, drill
    with ½" wood bit, sandpaper, dull pen-
    cil, waxed paper, paint brushes.

Transfer all patterns to wood, aligning
them with the grain of the wood according
to arrows on patterns. Cut around the outlines with either a band saw or jigsaw. Drill
through the two end pieces of the barn as
indicated on the pattern, using a ½" wood
bit. Sand all pieces smooth.

Transfer patterns for details to each animal. One of the easiest methods for doing
this is to trace the pattern with a dull pencil
onto waxed paper. Then place the waxed
paper over the wooden cut-out. Go back
over the lines again with the pencil, pressing
down hard enough to leave an impression
on the wood beneath. The impression then
serves as a guide for your painting. Paint the
animals as indicated on the patterns.

Assemble the barn by overlapping the two
end pieces over the long front and back
pieces. Run a thin line of glue along each
edge where the pieces will overlap; then nail
in place with at least three nails in each corner. Glue and nail hardboard to bottom.

Following the procedure given above,
transfer the details to the barn, and paint as
indicated on the pattern.

Insert the dowel through the holes on the
end pieces to form a carrying handle. Drive
a small nail through the top of barn into the
dowel to keep it from slipping out.

 ## POP-UP SANTA TOYS

Remember the days when toys moved on child-power and imagination instead of batteries? These peek-a-boo Pop-up Santa toys are the old-fashioned kind—made with simple scraps and lots of love. Younger children will amuse themselves by the hour as Santa disappears down the chimney, then POPS up to look around. Make an extra one or two so that your child and his little friends may use them for puppet shows.

YOU WILL NEED:
patterns on pages 140 and 141
quart-sized milk carton
felt in gray, red, black, white, pink
felt-tipped pen (black medium-point)
12" wooden paint stirrer
2" foam ball
household glue
red fabric scraps
1 pom-pom of ball fringe

Cut the milk carton to a height of 4". Cut gray felt 4" wide and long enough to wrap around your carton. With a felt-tipped pen, draw bricks on the felt.

Push the wooden stirrer into the foam ball, gluing it in place. Cut one strip of pink felt 3" x 1½". Glue onto front of ball for face, smoothing the edges to fit the contours.

Cut one hat and one body from red fabric. Cut fur for hat, buckle, two sleeve cuffs, snow for the chimney, beard, and mustache from white felt. Cut two hands from red felt. Cut belt from black felt.

Sew seam on hat with right sides together. Turn right side out and glue onto head. Glue the white felt fur over the edge of the hat, concealing raw edges of hat and face.

Slip the belt through the two slits of the buckle. Glue the belt across the front of the body. Pin the hands with straight edges lined up with the end of the sleeve, hands pointing toward center of body. With right sides together, sew side seams of the body, catching the hands and belt as you go. Turn right side out. Glue cuffs onto sleeves.

At the neck of the body (the "X" on the pattern), cut a slit just big enough to push the paint stirrer through. Slip the body over the stirrer and against the head. Tack the back of the body, at the neck, to the bottom of the hat. Run a ring of glue around the bottom of the head and on the right side of the neck. Slide your hand into the body and press the neck firmly against the bottom of the head. Allow to dry thoroughly.

Make a 1¼"-square hole in the exact center of the bottom of the milk carton; then push the end of the stirrer through this hole. Glue the bottom edge of the body on the outside of the carton, with the fabric covering the carton to a depth of ½". Glue the gray felt over the carton, hiding the edge of the body. Glue the snow around the top of the chimney; glue on beard, mustache, and eyes. Tack a pom-pom at the tip of the hat.

A CHRISTMAS JOURNAL

Don't you often wish that you had written down some of the happy things that happened in past holiday seasons? Remember the doll Aunt Mary gave to the baby, and how the baby laughed and held up her arms when she saw it? And where are the names and numbers of old friends you still call every Christmas? Somehow, memories have a way of dimming through the years, and numbers have a way of being misplaced—unless you have written them in a book.

Capture the memories in a special little journal, covered with fabric and decorated with a cross-stitched Santa. The book will become a priceless source of smiles—and hearty laughter—in years to come, as you read through the pages, and add to it each Christmas season.

YOU WILL NEED:
chart and color key on page 146
embroidery floss
#14 Aida cloth (6" x 6½" piece)
⅔ yd. red piping
blank book (6½" x 8½" or similar size)
⅓ yd. green polka-dot fabric
⅓ yd. iron-on interfacing
⅓ yd. (⅜"-wide) red grosgrain ribbon
2 small jingle bells
white household glue

Work the design in cross-stitch on the Aida cloth. Add the words "Best Wishes" in backstitch. Sew piping around the edges of the Aida cloth (on the right side, with raw edges of piping and Aida cloth together and to the outside.) Turn under the edge of the cloth and piping; then press.

Blank books come in a number of sizes; for a correct fit, measure the exact size of your book. Use the instructions given here to determine the size of the fabric piece you will cut for your particular book, even if it does not measure 6½" x 8½".

First, measure the height of your book. Add this measurement, ¼" extra for ease,

and two ½" seam allowances. (For example, on a book 8½" tall, you would add 8½", plus ¼", plus 1", for a total of 9¾".) This will be the measurement for the short side of the fabric cover.

To obtain the length, measure the width of your book carefully, then the width of the spine. Add four times the width (for front and back plus inside covers), the thickness of the spine, ¼" extra for ease, and two ½" allowances for turning under raw edges. Then subtract 1". (For example, on a book 6½" wide, you would add 26", plus the width of the spine which is ¾", plus ¼" ease, plus 1" for a total of 28". When you subtract 1", you arrive at 27".) The figure you get will be the length of the fabric needed for the cover. The correct measurement for a book 6½" x 8½" is 9¾" x 27".

Cut one rectangular piece of fabric to the size you have determined is correct for your book. Cut one piece of interfacing to this same size. Press with wrong sides together to form a bond. Turn under ½" at each short end, wrong sides together, and press.

Place cover right side up. Fold each end toward the center. (See diagram.) The amount folded in at each end should equal ½" less than the width of the book. Pin in place and stitch according to diagram. Press seams toward center, folding under ½" at the spine section so that raw edges will be hidden. Turn right side out and press again.

Slip the book cover into the case. Close the book; then center the piped cross-stitched panel on the front. Pin in place. Sew the panel on by hand with blind stitch.

Sew the bells to one end of the ribbon and glue the other end inside the spine at the top of the book.

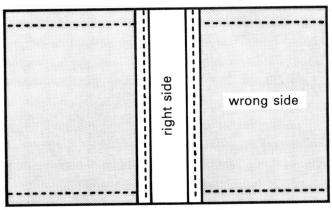

right side

wrong side

sew along broken lines

THE LITTLE TOY SOLDIER

This smart-stepping wooden soldier stands almost 19″ tall and is made with only three easy-to-cut pattern pieces. He can sit, stand at attention, or march right along a mantel or table at Christmastime. Kids will enjoy displaying him in their room during the rest of the year.

YOU WILL NEED:
patterns on page 142
1″ x 12″ x 18″ length of pine shelving without knotholes
semi-gloss spray varnish
gloss latex enamel or acrylic paints (black, white, red, yellow, brown, blue)
4½″ (⅜″-diameter) dowel
Have on hand: band saw or jigsaw, drill with ⅜″ wood bit, sandpaper, paint brushes, hammer

Transfer pattern to wood, making sure that the grain runs lengthwise on the pattern pieces. Cut around the outlines with a jigsaw or band saw. Mark the spots for the dowels (see the "Xs" on each pattern piece); then drill through the wood, using a ⅜″ wood bit. For a clean, non-splintered hole, place the wood over a piece of scrap lumber, and drill through into the bottom piece. Stop the drill before pulling it out of the hole, or the hole will become too large. Sand all edges and the surface.

Transfer patterns for details onto the wood. Spray over the markings with a thin coat of varnish to seal the wood and provide a better surface for painting. Paint on the details, starting with large areas of color and moving to smaller ones. You will need to mix the red and white paints to obtain a flesh tone. Allow to dry overnight.

Cut two 2¼″ lengths of dowel. Hammer one dowel through the legs and lower body and the other through the arms and upper body. Dowels must fit tightly or the movements of the arms and legs cannot be controlled. Touch up the paint over the dowel ends if desired.

STAINED GLASS
IN THE KITCHEN

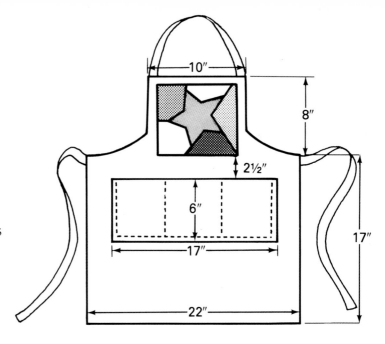

If Christmas always finds you in the kitchen, you can still be dressed for the season in this apron with its bib of appliquéd "stained glass." The matching potholder is oversized to hold even large casserole dishes comfortably.

YOU WILL NEED:
pattern on page 144
¾ yd. green pin-dot cotton-blend fabric
⅜ yd. gold cotton-blend fabric
⅜ yd. iron-on interfacing
water soluble stick glue (optional)
⅜ yd. paper for machine appliqué
⅜ yd. Pellon® fleece or polyester batting
2 yds. (⅝"-wide) grosgrain ribbon
scraps of red, purple, blue, gray, and orange fabric
green sewing thread

All fabrics you choose should have the same laundering instructions. Pre-wash and iron all fabrics before beginning.

APRON: Follow the diagram to make a pattern from newspaper or wrapping paper. Fold the pattern in half lengthwise before cutting to ensure equal sides. *Note that the diagram shows finished sizes only.* Allow an extra inch all around on both the body and pocket pieces for a double-turned edge. Cut one body piece and one pocket 18" x 7½" from the green pin-dot fabric. (See diagram.)

Make the body of the apron by folding under all edges twice, pressing, then stitching. To make the pocket, fold over the top edge twice to make a ½"-wide hem. Stitch to hold. Turn under ½" on both bottom and sides; then press. Fold into thirds and press to make guide lines for sewing. Pin pocket onto apron, and stitch in place on both sides, bottom, and along fold lines to make three separate sections.

Cut shapes indicated on pattern from fabric scraps that have been reinforced with iron-on interfacing. Arrange the appliqué pieces on the bib, with edges touching. Pin or glue (with water soluble stick glue) in place. Pin a piece of paper for machine appliqué to the back of the bib. Stitch over the edge of each piece to join all layers, using a medium-wide zigzag satin stitch. There will be a double row of green stitching between colors. Tear away the paper backing.

Cut three 22"-long pieces of ribbon. Sew one to the corners of the bib for a neck strap, turning under ends. Fold under ½" at one end of each of the other ribbons. Attach these ends at apron corners to form ties.

POTHOLDER: Cut one 10" square from both the gold and the green pin-dot fabric. Cut two 10" squares of Pellon® fleece or polyester batting. Reinforce fabric scraps for appliqué with iron-on interfacing, and cut shapes according to pattern.

Center the appliqué design on the right side of the green square and pin in place. Appliqué as instructed for the apron.

Cut a 6" length of ribbon and fold to form a loop. Sew to one corner of the front, with loop pointing towards center. Place the gold back on the appliquéd front, right sides together. Place one square of fleece batting on each side. Pin together and stitch through all 4 layers with a ¼" seam around edges, leaving a 3" opening for turning.

Turn right sides out, and close opening by hand. Machine quilt with a straight stitch on the border and between the double rows of satin stitching.

FOLK-ART SEWING BASKET

If you are partial to folk embroidery because of its exuberant colors and intricate designs, you'll take special pleasure in making this basket with its bright flowers and curling tendrils. Ideal for holding sewing supplies or those tiny treasures everyone seems to accumulate, this practical basket will enhance any dresser. The friend or relative who receives one as a gift will know just how much love went into making it.

A purchased basket forms the base for the embroidered and padded lid, while colorful braid trimming adds the final touch.

YOU WILL NEED:
pattern and color key on page 143
8" x 10" piece of linen (ecru)
transfer pencil, tracing paper or other
   means of transferring design to fabric
embroidery flosses
oval, woven-grass basket with a lid (about
   7½" long)
8" x 10" piece of polyester fleece

⅔ yd. (1"-wide) embroidered tape
⅔ yd. (½"-wide) embroidered tape
white household glue

Transfer design to fabric. Use 4 strands of floss unless otherwise indicated.

Work vines and tendrils in backstitch, ending each "curl" with a French knot. Work leaves, hearts, and bird's head in satin stitch. Work the inner pink layer on the lower pink flowers in 2 rows of backstitch; work the other layers in satin stitch. Work the remaining flowers in satin stitch.

Work the flower stamens with 1 strand of black floss in long, straight stitches, topped with 2 French knots on pink flowers and 1 French knot on blue flowers. Work pink buds (circles) in padded satin stitch and small blue buds and blue dots on bird's head in single French knots.

To work the lattice in the centers of the yellow flowers, first work the center in orange satin stitch. Then, using 1 strand of black floss, work a lattice in long, straight stitches, first in one direction, then the opposite. Make a tiny straight stitch over each intersection with 1 strand of light yellow floss.

Work the bird's body and comb in split stitch and the tail feathers in satin stitch. Work the wing in backstitch.

Using 2 strands of floss, work beak and eyes in satin stitch. Outline the bird in backstitch with 1 strand of black floss.

Block the finished stitchery. Trace around the basket lid onto the polyester fleece. Cut fleece along tracing line. Center the lid over the back of the embroidered design, and trace around the lid onto the fabric. Draw a second line ½" outside the first line. Cut along the outside line, and clip every ½" almost to the first outline, forming "tabs" all around the edge. Place the fleece oval over the oval tracing on the fabric back. Spread a thin layer of glue on the edge of the basket lid. Position the lid over the fleece oval, and bring up the fabric "tabs," pressing them onto the glued edge of the lid. Glue 1"-wide trim to the lid edge and ½"-wide trim to the bottom edge of the basket.

THIS DOLL IS A SOFTIE

Little mommies can love and care for this doll to their heart's content, and their own mothers can relax, knowing the doll has no buttons or other trim that a child might swallow. Made from a single sock and dressed with scraps left over from your own child's dress, this gentle doll is sure to be cuddled Christmas night—and long after.

YOU WILL NEED:
pattern on page 145
1 toddler's size 7-7½ ankle sock, cotton or cotton blend
white sewing thread
polyester stuffing
1-ounce skein of yellow baby yarn
5" x 7" piece of cardboard
embroidery floss—small amount of light blue, light brown, and rose pink
powdered blush
remnant of fabric for dress and panties
elastic thread
12" lace for collar

The doll is made from one sock with no black-stamped markings, using the toe for the head and the heel for the doll's bottom. Arms are made from the top 2½" of the sock and legs from the remaining portion of the ankle.

Cut off the 2½" portion allowed for the arms, and cut along the knitted ribs to form two equal pieces. Fold each of these pieces in half lengthwise, right sides together, and seam along the side and the end with the raw edges. Turn right side out, fill with stuffing, and whipstitch to close.

Stuff the foot of the sock firmly for the doll's head and body. Place the sock with the toe pointing straight up. Starting at the raw edge, make a 2" cut through the center of both layers of the ankle to form the legs. Blindstitch the inside seams of the legs together beginning at the crotch, but leaving the ends of the tubes open. Stuff the tubes; then close the ends by placing a line of running stitches around the edge and gathering.

To form the doll's head, make a line of running stitches approximately 3" from the toe going completely around the sock. Pull on the thread until the desired shape is obtained, and tack in place. Wrap thread around the neck several times before tying off. Stitch arms in place ½" below the neckline, finished edge turned toward the body.

For the hair, wrap baby yarn firmly, but not tightly, around the long side of the cardboard. Secure the yarn at one end of the cardboard with backstitch to form a part. Cut yarn loose on the opposite end.

Center the hair on the doll's head and stitch in place along the part, using the same yarn. Make bangs to cover the forehead by wrapping yarn around two fingers fifteen times. Tie one end and clip the other. Fasten the resulting bunch to the head at the beginning of the part. Make a bow from a strip of dress fabric, and tack in place.

Lightly mark facial features with a soft pencil. Embroider, using blue satin stitch for the eyes, brown outline stitch for the brows, and pink outline stitch for the mouth. Dab a tiny amount of powdered blush onto the cheeks and bridge of the nose.

Cut 2 sleeve pieces and 2 dress pieces. Join sleeves to dress pieces with a ¼" seam, matching letters as shown on the pattern. Sew the side and underarm seams in one operation. Turn under neck and sleeve openings ⅛", then ⅛" again, and press. Hem the neck with machine stitching, using elastic thread on the bobbin. Hem the armholes in the same manner. Stretch the neck out, and sew ungathered lace to the upper edge of the neck opening by hand. Finish the bottom of the dress with a 1" hem.

Cut one piece to make the panties. Take two small tucks on each side of the back of the panties as indicated on the pattern. Fold the panties, right side together, and machine stitch the side seams. Sew a small hem along the panty legs and the waist, again using elastic thread on the bobbin so that legs and waist will be gathered.

RAINY DAY FUN FOLDER

This neat little folder contains everything needed to keep your child happily occupied on a rainy afternoon or a big day at Grandmother's house. Well-stocked with an assortment of crayons, paints, paper, and books (each in its own little pocket), the activity folder will stimulate creativity and encourage constructive play.

YOU WILL NEED:
patterns for heart appliqués on page 132
⅔ yd. plaid cotton or cotton flannel
2 (2½" x 26") pieces denim
6 squares felt in colors to blend with
    plaid fabric
14" x 21" polyester batting
2" Velcro® tape
transparent sewing thread
activity supplies: 2 coloring or drawing
    books; 12" ruler; selection of paints,
    crayons, markers, pencils, scissors

From the plaid fabric, cut two 14" x 21" pieces and two 14" x 9" pieces. Prepare large pockets by hemming one long side of each of the 14" x 9" pieces. Arrange the craft supplies, except for coloring books and ruler, on these large pockets, making sure first that the hemmed side of each pocket is down. Cut additional pockets from felt in sizes needed to hold the smaller supplies, adding ¼" seam allowances around the sides of each pocket. Cut simple appliqués such as the hearts shown here and sew these to some of the pockets. Sew the felt pockets to the larger plaid pockets; the tops of the felt pockets should be turned in the opposite direction from the hemmed edges of the large pockets.

Place the plaid pockets at each end of one of the large pieces of plaid—with right sides up, hems toward center, and raw edges of the plaid pockets even with raw edges of the large piece of plaid. Baste around the edge, with a ½" seam allowance. This should form two compartments for coloring books.

To make the handles, fold each of the denim pieces lengthwise, with right sides together. Stitch along the raw edge, using a ¼" seam. Turn and press. Position the two handles on the right side of the remaining 14" x 21" piece of fabric. Pin the handles in place, letting the loops extend past the raw edges. Sew around the ends of the handles to secure, without getting into the ½" seam allowance. Cut felt appliqués and place them over the raw ends of the handles. Stitch in place with transparent thread. Fold both loops back toward the center, and pin in place before proceeding.

Place the piece of batting on a flat surface. Place the plaid piece with pockets, right side up, on the batting. Place remaining large piece of fabric (with pinned-back handles) on top, wrong side up. Pin. Sew through all thicknesses, around all edges except for an opening for turning. Turn and press. Whip-stitch opening closed.

Cut a piece of felt that is 9" long and 1¾" wide. Center this on inside of folder between pockets to form a spine along the bottom of the folder. Pin felt in place, and stitch in place along both sides, continuing the rows of stitching to the outside edges of the folder. When a 12" ruler is slipped into this pocket, it will add support to the bottom. Sew small squares of Velcro® tape to the inside corners of the folder for closure.

TELL A SIMPLE STORY

Despite the whirl of activity surrounding the season, it is important to remind children of the true meaning of Christmas and why it is celebrated. Sometimes a simple nativity scene tells the story best, in a way that even a small child understands.

These nativities are made from flour, salt, and water—mixed to form a type of bread dough just right for molding figures. Two examples are shown—a small one that is both colorful and whimsical, and a larger one that is left natural and unadorned. Basic methods for making any bread dough nativity are the same, yet each will be unique.

YOU WILL NEED:
1 cup salt
1 cup warm water (or slightly more if necessary)
4 cups all-purpose flour
spray varnish
optional: aluminum foil, water color paints and brushes, fine marking pens, wooden round, white household glue

Place salt and water in a blender and mix at highest speed for two minutes. Pour into a bowl and add a little flour at a time. Knead with your hands until the dough is smooth and soft, not granular and no longer sticky. Keep it in a plastic bag in the refrigerator until ready to use.

Mold the figures directly on a cookie sheet covered with aluminum foil. Individual parts of each figure are stuck together with water. To attach heavier pieces, break a toothpick in half and push it into the figure to hold the parts in place until baking is complete. (If the end of a toothpick protrudes, it may be cut off later.)

Make the bodies from dough rolled between the hands to form a thick coil. Form heads from balls of dough; stick onto the bodies with water. Smaller coils of dough become the arms. To make flat sheets (for headdresses and robes) roll the dough with a rolling pin dusted with flour. Shape other pieces, such as mushrooms or strawberries, from flattened balls of dough.

Larger figures, such as those left natural in the photograph, would be too thick to bake properly if they were solid dough. Instead, the inside of each figure is filled with aluminum foil. To make similar figures, use a roll of foil for the body, and a ball of foil for the head. Cover with bread dough, join with water and/or toothpicks, and bend the body into shape. Prop the figures with additional foil if necessary while baking.

Many household implements may be used to mark the dough while it is still soft. Try making indentations with a toothpick or the point of a small knife. Hair, or straw, is made by squeezing a ball of dough through a garlic press. To make tiny cuts between fingers or on leaves at the top of strawberries, use cuticle scissors.

In most cases, the figures should be baked in a very slow oven (250°) until completely hard. Depending on the size of the figures, this could take up to 3 hours. If you would like a browned appearance on figures which are not to be painted, turn the temperature to 300° during the last half of baking.

After the dough has cooled, the figures may be painted. Watercolor paints were used to decorate the nativity scene on the wooden round (see photograph). Acrylic paints might also be used for a more opaque appearance. Let the paint dry before adding details with a felt-tipped marking pen.

Whether the figures are painted or not, they *must* be given a protective coat of varnish in order to keep out moisture in the air. Spray on several very thin coats to cover each figure completely.

Display the varnished figures dramatically against a backdrop of rocks or greenery, or mount them on a base. If a wooden base is used, glue the bottom of each figure directly onto the wood. Decorate with moss and small dried flowers if you wish.

NUTTY CHRISTMAS CRITTERS

Clear the way for this zany group of Christmas Critters—all made with nuts and guaranteed to produce smiles or even gales of giggles from your children. From the bucktoothed Mouse made from a walnut to the feisty Porcupine with his chestnut body and long black whiskers, every ornament is loaded with personality.

Each wide-eyed critter has different features made from snips of felt and leather, but they all favor wearing the same red hat for the holidays.

YOU WILL NEED:
patterns on page 146
purchased eyes
glue
specific materials listed below

RED SANTA HAT: (worn by all the critters)
felt in red and white
white fringe (about 15 threads)
6" gold thread

Cut hat from red felt and hat band from white felt. Place fringe at small end of hat so that woven side of fringe extends beyond edge. Fold hat lengthwise, right sides together. Sew hat across top and down side, catching fringe in place. Turn right side out. Fold hat band end to end; sew across ends. Turn band right side out, and slide over hat. Attach hats to critters with glue, securing both hat and band firmly. Fold hat in half, with point down. Using gold thread and a large-eyed needle, sew through the fold once and make a loop for hanging.

PENGUIN:
pecan
black paint
felt in black, orange,
   and white

Paint pecan black, and allow to dry. Cut feet and beak from orange felt, front of penguin from white felt, and 2 wings from black felt. Using the photograph as a guide to placement, glue feet to bottom of nut, front of penguin to front of nut, wings at sides of white front, beak at top of white front, and eyes just above the beak. Add a Santa hat.

MOUSE:
small block of plastic foam
green foil wrapping paper
red yarn
brown felt or leather
half walnut shell
thin white cardboard
heavy black thread
peppercorn

To make the present that is the base, wrap the plastic foam in green foil paper and tie with red yarn. Cut a tail from brown felt. Glue the tail to the inside of the walnut, with the tail extending behind the body. Run a line of glue around the rim of the walnut and place on top of the wrapped package.

Cut 2 teeth from white cardboard. Cut 2 ears and 2 cheeks from brown felt. Using the photograph as a guide to placement, add teeth, cheeks, whiskers (two 1½"-long pieces of heavy thread), a peppercorn nose, the eyes, the ears, and a red Santa hat.

BLUE BIRD:
pecan
filbert
orange felt
blue felt or leather

Glue filbert to top of one end of the pecan; hold in place until dry or use quick-setting hot glue from a glue gun. Cut 1 tail and 2 wings from blue felt and 1 beak from orange. Using the photograph as a guide to placement, glue tail, wings, beak and eyes in place; top with a red Santa hat.

PORCUPINE:
chestnut hull
center from a black-eyed Susan
heavy black thread
black seed or bead
brown felt or leather

The chestnut should be picked from the tree while it is still green so the hull will not open. Glue the center from the black-eyed Susan in place for the snout. Cut whiskers (3 pieces of heavy black thread 1½"-long), and glue at end of snout. Glue black seed or bead at very tip of snout. Glue on eyes. Cut a brown felt tail from same pattern as the one given for the mouse. Glue in place, and add a red Santa hat.

LION:
large pecan or long acorn
Canadian thistle or large straw flower
light brown felt or leather
felt in white and red
white fringe
heavy black thread
peppercorn
2 gold pipe cleaners
cocklebur

Glue the center of the thistle to the end of the pecan or acorn. Allow to dry.

Cut 1 face and 2 ears of brown felt, then 2 cheeks of white felt, and a mouth of red felt. Cut three 1"-long pieces of black thread for whiskers and a snip of fringe for the beard. Using the photograph as a guide to placement, glue the facial features on the front of the thistle. Add the eyes, a pepper-corn for the nose, and ears above the face.

For the tail, cut a 2"-long piece of pipe cleaner; twist it to curl and glue a cocklebur to one end. Attach tail to end of body with glue and allow to dry.

For the legs, cut four 1"-long pieces of pipe cleaner. Bend each into an "L" shape so the legs curve forward for feet. Glue to bottom of nut. Glue hat to top of nut, placing it just behind the thistle.

67

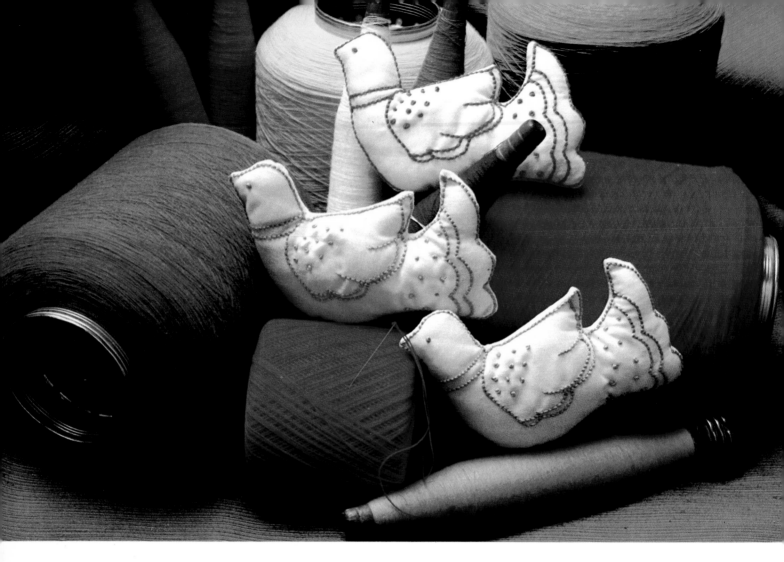

 # EMBROIDERED DOVES

Traditional symbols of peace, these plump white doves are worked in easy embroidery stitches. Their only color comes from French knot and backstitch details—making these birds just right for an old-fashioned tree where more elaborate ornaments would seem quite out of place. Mix potpourri with the stuffing and they become sweet sachets for a special friend's closet.

YOU WILL NEED:
pattern on page 143
removable marker
2 (7" squares) cotton or cotton-blend
  fabric for each bird
cotton embroidery floss
polyester stuffing
nylon thread or dental floss

Transfer the pattern to one square of the fabric with a removable marker. Do not cut out yet. Using six strands of floss, work all solid lines, including the outlines of the bird, in backstitch. Work dots on the tail, wing, and eye in French knots.

Place the finished embroidery and backing fabric with right sides together. Sew the two layers together very close (about 1/16") to the backstitched outlines of the bird, either by hand or with the zipper foot on the sewing machine; leave an opening for stuffing.

Trim excess fabric to within ¼" of the stitching and clip the seam allowance at curves. Turn the dove right side out and stuff. Slip stitch the opening to close. Attach a loop of nylon thread or dental floss to the tip of the wing for hanging.

GLITTERING NEEDLEPOINT

Needlepoint has never sparkled like this! Worked in a mixture of tapestry wool and metallic yarns on golden-toned canvas, the richly textured ornaments are stunning against a background of greenery.

Though three separate designs are given, the front and back of each is different. All three ornaments can be made from a single 9″ x 12″ sheet of metallic needlepoint canvas. This is a fairly new product—ask for it in your needlework shop.

YOU WILL NEED:
charts and color key on page 147
gold metallic needlepoint canvas
metallic needlepoint yarns in gold and
   silver
tapestry wool in red, dark green, light
   green, gold, ecru, black
#18 tapestry needle
green felt

Work the designs according to the charts, using a half-cross stitch throughout. Carefully cut out all the pieces, leaving one thread of canvas outside the stitched outlines. For each ornament, cut a piece of green felt slightly smaller than the canvas. (For the stocking ornament, which is left open at the top, cut two pieces of felt.) Sandwich the felt between the back and the front during assembly. Assemble the ornament by whipping the pieces together with gold metallic yarn over the outer threads of the canvas. Make a loop for hanging from gold yarn.

HOLIDAY GOODY BASKETS

Christmas is a good time to make use of baskets as containers for other gifts, especially those from your kitchen. Many stores sell a variety of interestingly shaped wooden baskets—all awaiting your special touch.

Simple motifs with acrylic paints and a paintbrush require no great artistic talent, yet the finished baskets look special indeed. Personalize them or write holiday messages with thin paint or ink. Your friends may eat the gift itself, but they'll enjoy its "wrapping" for years.

WRAPS WITH A PERSONAL STAMP

Invite the children to help you make this easiest-of-all gift wrap from brown paper—using an eraser for a stamp! You, Mommy, will need to cut the stamp, but the little ones can do the rest all by themselves.

Happy holly leaf designs will brighten up even the plainest basket, too, so that it's a fitting container for your best goodies. (See the recipe on page 92 for these delicious old-fashioned popcorn balls.)

YOU WILL NEED:
gum eraser and new pencil eraser
craft knife
ink, tempera, or artist's acrylic paints
brown paper or basket

Draw a holly leaf on a gum eraser. Cut around the outline of the leaf; then cut away the background, so that the leaf design is raised. Remove a strip for the leaf detail. The stamp for the holly berries is simply the eraser on a new pencil.

Ink, tempera, or artist's acrylics may be used equally well on paper, but the paint works best on the basket. Press the stamps into paint or inks and stamp the design onto the paper or basket.

HOT ROLLS COMING UP

This happy snowman will deliver piping
hot rolls to your table every time. And because he's worked in snowy white counted
cross-stitch, he'll never melt away but will
reappear at your table every holiday season.
You may even like to work this design on a
matching apron bib or kitchen towel.

YOU WILL NEED:
chart and color key on page 150
½ yd. (45"-wide) washable fabric
#14 Aida cloth (7" x 8½" piece)
embroidery floss (in colors indicated by
    color key)
jumbo rickrack

Work the snowman in cross-stitch on Aida
cloth. Use 3 strands of floss in the colors
suggested on the chart.

To make the bread warmer, cut the fabric
into two 16" x 22½" pieces. Fold each piece
in half (to 8" x 22½"), with right sides together. Machine stitch along the three unfin-
ished sides of each, leaving a small opening
for turning. Turn each piece right side out,
slip stitch the opening, and press flat.

Lay one of the finished fabric rectangles
on top of the other so that the two form a
cross. Machine stitch a square in the center
where the two pieces overlap.

Stitch the finished snowman panel to one
flap of the bread warmer. Sew on rickrack to
cover raw edges of the Aida cloth.

CITY GIRL & COUNTRY COUSIN

Whether your favorite little girl lives in the country or in the city—this flip-flop doll is the one she'll love! On one side is a prim city miss dressed in lacy pink with ribbons, while on the other is her fresh-faced country cousin wearing calico and a sunbonnet.

The patterns for this doll are simple; in fact, the dress skirt and the apron skirt are rectangles cut to measure and don't even require a pattern. Dress the doll as suggested, or use fabrics to match your child's room. Either way, this doll will be one to treasure, and chances are that she'll be passed down to another little girl some day.

YOU WILL NEED:
patterns on pages 148 and 149
⅓ yd. creamy white fabric
embroidery floss (small amounts of brown, pink, and blue)
polyester stuffing
⅔ yd. pink striped fabric
remnant of brown checked fabric
⅔ yd. brown calico
2¼ yds. (1"-wide) pregathered white lace
1½ yds. (¼"-wide) pink satin ribbon for skirt and braids

1 yd. (1"-wide) pink satin ribbon for sash
⅔ yd. (⅛"-wide) brown ribbon for bonnet
yarn for hair

Cut 2 doubled-ended doll heads, 4 arms, and 8 hands from creamy white fabric.

Unfold the doll heads and at each end of one head piece, embroider the faces. Use satin stitch in pink for both mouths, satin stitch in brown for eyes of country doll, satin stitch in blue for eyes of city doll, outline stitch in brown for top of eyes and eyebrows of both dolls, straight stitch in brown for nose of both dolls. Press.

Place hands with right sides together and sew, leaving wrist open. Clip curves, turn, and press. Stuff firmly. Fold arm pieces at fold line, and sew long sides. Slip hand into arm, right sides together, raw edges aligned, and thumb pointing up. Sew across wrist seam, through all thicknesses. Turn and press. Stuff arm only slightly; baste closed. Pin arms to body back piece, having arms toward center of back. Pin body front piece over back, right sides together. Sew around body and heads, leaving an opening on one side for turning. Clip curves, turn, and press. Stuff and close.

CLOTHING: For the city side of the doll, cut the following pieces from pink material: 1 dress bodice, 2 sleeves, 2 back facings, and a 36" x 14" rectangular skirt.

For the country side of the doll, cut the following pieces from creamy white fabric: 2 apron tops, 2 apron sashes (18" x 2½"), and 1 apron skirt (18" x 10"). From the brown checked fabric, cut 2 (2½" x 2½") pockets, 1 bonnet ruffle, 1 bonnet crown, and 2 bonnet brims. From the brown calico, cut 1 dress bodice, 2 back facings, 1 neck ruffle, 2 sleeves, and a 36" x 14" skirt.

DRESSES: With right sides together, sew facing to back opening of bodice. Fold facing to inside along fold line and sew in place. Finish neck by adding fabric ruffle for country side and lace ruffle for city side.

Turn under sleeve edge along hem line and stitch. Gather upper sleeve between notches. Match sleeve notches to those on bodice, adjust gathers, and sew. Press seam toward sleeve. Sew underarm seams, right sides together, stopping at seam line of dress bodice (dots on pattern). Turn, and press.

Sew back seam in skirt. Turn under ¼" along hem line and stitch. Sew ruffles, ribbon, and trims in place on city dress, extending bottom ruffle beyond hem.

Gather 2 rows around top edge of skirt. Mark center and sides of skirt. Gather. Pin dress bodice to skirt with right sides together, overlapping facings at bodice back to match back seam in skirt. Match sides and center front; adjust gathers. Sew around, stop at underarm seam, and start again on the other side of seam. Press.

Put dresses on dolls. Secure at neck openings. Pin waistlines to dolls and sew dresses to doll body at waistline seams. Match hemlines and pin. Turn under edges of both hemlines, and sew together. Tie ribbon sash around waist and ribbons around wrists to gather sleeves on city doll.

APRON: Sew apron top pieces together, right sides facing. Leave waistline seam open for turning. Turn and press.

Make patch pockets and attach to apron skirt. Hem skirt at sides and bottom. Gather top edge of skirt to width of apron top. Turn ¼" on apron top opening to inside and press. Insert gathered skirt into apron top opening and pin. Stitch apron top to skirt across opening, through all thicknesses. Top stitch around entire apron top. Fold sash pieces lengthwise with right sides together and sew. Turn right side out and press. Make a pleat in open end of sash. Pin pleated sash to side of apron top and sew in place. Fold under 1" on end of each strap and sew, forming a loop. Put apron on doll, crisscrossing straps in back. Run sashes through loops and tie in a bow.

BONNET: Sew brim pieces along curved side, right sides together. Clip, turn, and press. Gather bonnet crown around curve between dots. Match dots to brim, adjust gathers, and sew brim to crown. Fold ruffle lengthwise. Sew side seams. Turn and press. Gather along top edges. Pin ruffle to crown, matching dots and adjusting gathers to fit; then stitch. Sew ribbons to bonnet for ties.

HAIR: The hair is sewn to the head in sections. Cut several strands of yarn about 5" long. Using matching thread, sew through the center of these strands to the center back of head. Bring ends around to side seams and sew. Continue cutting 5" strands, sewing in place until the back of the head is covered. Trim any yarn ends that extend over side seams.

Cut strands about 16" long and sew to center of head as before. Do not attach at sides. Continue until top of head is covered. On each side, divide loose ends into 3 sections and braid. Tie end of braid with yarn. Trim ends. Repeat for other doll. To finish country side, bring braids to sides to cover seams and sew in place. For city side, form braids into loops and sew in place. Make ribbon bows and sew over braided loops.

Cover the work surface with newspapers. Cut the sides off the plastic meat containers, so that remaining surface is smooth. Place a cookie cutter on the plastic, and press down firmly to imprint the design without cutting through.

Squeeze ink onto a cookie sheet or other smooth surface. Roll over and over with the brayer until the entire brayer is evenly coated with a thin film of lump-free ink. Roll the brayer over the imprinted plastic to coat it completely with ink (see photograph). The imprint will show up against the color, since it does not become coated.

COOKIE-CUTTER BLOCK PRINTS

Children love the idea of making their own cards and gift wrap at Christmastime. Here's a way to let them do it with minimum fuss—and absolutely terrific results.

Basic block printing techniques, greatly simplified, are used to decorate any kind of paper or cardboard. Even a small child can participate in many of the steps.

Plastic meat containers with cookie cutter designs pressed into them form the print blocks. Ink is applied and the block is pressed onto paper to make holiday prints.

YOU WILL NEED:
clean plastic foam meat containers
cookie cutters in holiday shapes
waterbased ink for block printing
brayer—found in art stores
lunch bags, construction paper, etc.

Turn the block over and place it on the paper. Firmly rub the back of the block with the heel of your hand to transfer the design. Lift the block straight up; then set the print aside to dry. Each block may be reused many times, but it should be recoated with fresh ink before each printing.

Some meat containers have an embossed texture (see photograph) for making backgrounds or details in a different color.

Other details may be made by writing (backwards so that it appears correctly in the finished print) or drawing on the plastic with a dull pencil.

UP, UP & AWAY

Traveling is a pleasure with these handy calico and ribbon shoe bags, which hold a pair apiece, and a quilted hosiery case to keep your hose from snagging. The well-stocked sewing kit makes even a pulled hem only a minor mishap.

Make these accessories from several coordinating print fabrics in colors to go with the luggage. Add matching ribbons and seam bindings for a tailored, yet feminine, touch.

The little hot-air-balloon design is made using a very old quilt technique—the gathered yo-yo—appliquéd onto the front of both the hosiery and sewing cases. Fill the balloons with your favorite potpourri to give the whole suitcase a wonderful fresh scent.

YOU WILL NEED:

⅔ yd. double-sided quilted fabric (for
    sewing kit and hosiery case)
⅔ yd. of print fabric (for two shoe bags)
2 (14½″ x 13″) pieces of coordinating print
    fabrics (hosiery case)
3 yds. (½″ diameter) grosgrain ribbon
2 skeins embroidery floss in coordinating
    colors (for balloons)
scraps of basket-weave fabric (for balloon
    gondolas)
1 package double-fold seam binding
potpourri (to fill balloons)

SHOE BAGS: For each bag, cut a strip of
fabric 32″ x 12″. Fold fabric end to end,
right sides together. Starting at the bottom
fold, sew side seams of bag with a ½″ seam,
stopping 4″ from raw edges. Press the seams
open, turning under the remaining raw edges
at the side ½″.

To make casings along each top edge, turn
under fabric ½″, then 1½″. Sew two lines of
stitching on each side, one along the bottom
edge of the casing and the other ½″ toward
the folded edge. Insert 30″ of ribbon through
the casing.

SEWING CASE: Cut quilted fabric 8¼″ x
5½″. Place 2 strips of ribbon across fabric,
1½″ and 2¼″ from one end. Sew across
ends of ribbons. Wrap thread around one
ribbon; tack buttons and hook-and-eye to the
other ribbon. Cut one 2½″-long ribbon for
scissors holder, sewing the center of ribbon
to fabric. Turn under ends of ribbon and sew
on a snap at each end (see photograph).

Pin an 8″-long ribbon to each end of the
case with one end of ribbons even with the
raw edges, and the other pointing towards
the center of the case. Cover edges with bias
binding, catching the ribbon. Make balloon
as explained for Hosiery Case. Furnish case
with needles, pins, scissors, and buttons.

HOSIERY CASE: Cut double-face quilted
fabric 20″ x 10″. From each of two printed
fabrics, cut a piece 14½″ x 13″. Place the
printed fabrics right sides together, and sew
along the two 13″ sides. Turn and press.
Mark the center lines, vertically and horizontally, with pins. Mark the lengthwise center
line of the quilted fabric with pins. Place
one seamed edge of the printed fabric ¾″
from one edge of the shorter side of the
quilted fabric. Match the lengthwise center
lines of both printed and quilted fabrics, and
sew along that line. (Figure 1.) Match the
outside edges of the printed and quilted fabrics along the side of the bag and sew.

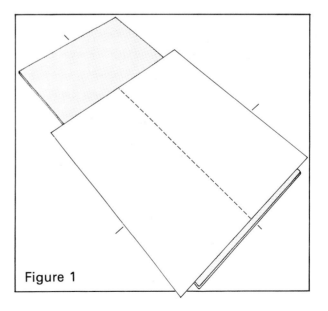

Figure 1

Form the pockets by making an inverted double pleat at the center and a single inverted pleat at each side, equalizing the depth of the pleats. Press in place. Sew across all pleats along the crosswise center line of the printed fabric. (Figure 2.)

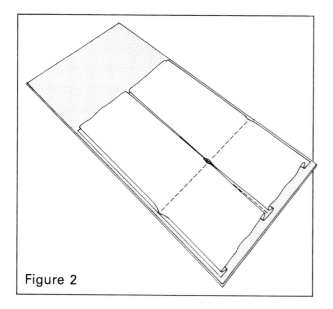

Figure 2

Pin one 12" length of ribbon to outside center of quilted fabric on the end of the bag away from the pockets, turning the ribbon toward the center of the bag. Bind edges of bag with bias binding, catching ribbon.

Cut balloons (3½" circles) from printed fabrics. Gather around the edge with a running stitch, fill loosely with potpourri, and pull thread to close. Appliqué the balloons in place, gathered edges down. For each balloon, cut three (6" long) lengths of 6-strand embroidery floss. Fold all three in half, and knot all of them together about ¼" below the fold. Place this center knot at the top of the balloon, pinning in place.

For each balloon, cut one gondola (1½" x 1¼" with ¼" turned under on all sides). Pin the gondola in place. Couch the floss into place with a single strand of matching floss. Appliqué gondola, hiding ends of floss.

Fold the bag along the seam between pockets. Fold over the flap. Add another 12" length of ribbon to match the first tie, stitching it in place.

GIFTS FOR THE MAN WHO TRAVELS

When a man travels away from home, small comforts mean a lot. These handsome travel accessories will organize his belongings and remind him of you each time he opens his suitcase.

There are two roomy shoe bags, a quilted case to keep his ties folded neatly, and even a tiny sewing kit—in case a button pops off just before an important meeting.

YOU WILL NEED:
2 yds. each (1"-wide and ½"-wide) grosgrain ribbon
1 yd. fabric (for two shoe bags)
2 extra long shoestrings (for shoe bags)
⅓ yd. double-sided quilted fabric (for tie case and sewing kit)
accessories for sewing kit (needles, thread, scissors, buttons)
1 package double-fold seam binding
3 large snaps (or pairs of Velcro® dots)

Begin by preparing a double-layered trimming from the two different widths of ribbons. Cut a 37"-long strip from each ribbon.

Center the narrow ribbon on the wider one and stitch along both edges of the narrow ribbon. This trimming will be used in making the closures for both the sewing kit and the tie case. Set aside until ready to use.

SHOE BAGS: For each shoe bag, cut one piece of fabric 34" x 15". Assemble as directed for the woman's shoe bag (on page 77), but use an extra-long shoestring as the tie for the bag.

SEWING CASE: Cut one piece of quilted fabric 5" x 3½". Cut a 3½"-long piece of (½"-wide) ribbon and tack both ends to the inside edges of the case (see photograph). Wrap the ribbon with threads in basic colors, tack on a shirt button, and add two needles—already threaded.

Cut a 7"-long strip of the double ribbon trim. Place it lengthwise on the outside of the case, with one end even with the bottom raw edge and the other end extending over the case. Stitch across the ribbon to hold it in place (at the exact middle of the case, and then ½" in from both raw edges). Sew bias binding around all edges. Turn under ribbon flap ½", and add a snap for closure.

TIE CASE: Cut one piece of quilted fabric to 17½" x 12". Cut two 15" lengths of the double ribbon trim. Turn under 1" at one end of each, and sew in place. Pin the other end of both ribbon trims to the edge of the case on the outside. Position the ribbon trims 4" from each end of the case, with the turned-under ends toward the inside. Top-stitch the overlapping ends of the ribbons about ½" from the edge of the case to hold in place.

On the inside of the case, pin a 12"-long piece of narrow ribbon across the fabric, 6" from one end. Pin the wider ribbon (12" long with 1" turned under on both ends) approximately 2½" from the opposite end of the case. Sew a row of stitching down the exact center of the tie case, catching the ribbons on both sides of the case beneath the stitching. Add fasteners (either snaps or Velcro® dots) to each end of the wider ribbon and to the fabric beneath. On each edge of the narrow ribbon, make some little tacks by hand, about one inch on each side of the center line. Make more tacks 1½" in from the raw edges.

Bind the edges with bias binding. Add fasteners to overlapping ends of the ribbon trim, close the case, and add fasteners on opposite ends of the ribbon.

FRISKY ROPE HORSES

If holiday shopping has you galloping all over town, take a few minutes to sit—and make these very easy, inexpensive rope horses. The time you spend creating them will relax you, and your kids will love playing with them.

Standing only 4" high, these ponies are just the right size to scamper across a table or mantel or even to hang on your tree. The colorful saddles and other trimmings are made from felt and bits of braid. Wire twisted around the rope lets you bend them any way you wish.

YOU WILL NEED (to make one horse):
20" (⅜"-diameter) sisal rope
18" floral wire (thin gauge)
scraps of black felt and other colors
thread
hot glue or household cement

Cut the rope into three pieces—two pieces 5½" long for the legs, and one piece 9" long for the body, tail and head. Cut floral wire to the same lengths as the short ropes, but two inches shorter (7") than the long one. Twist wire around each of the three pieces

so that it is almost hidden in the spirals of the rope. Fold back the unwired two inches of the long rope and hold in place to form a head. Wrap thread tightly around the head about ½" from the tip of the nose and then 1" further back. Hold the thread in place with a dab of glue. Wrap more thread (and glue) around this same piece of rope about ¾" from the other end, unraveling the end after the glue dries.

Approximately ½" from each end of the two short pieces, wrap thread tightly around the rope, dabbing with glue.

Place the three wired pieces of rope on waxed paper, with the long one in the middle. All three ropes should be even at the tail end. The long rope should be positioned so that the folded-back head is on the top. Glue all three pieces together at the midpoint of the short pieces. Let glue dry with the ropes still flat and side by side.

Cut one piece of felt 1" x 3" (for the saddle), one piece ⅓" x 2" (for the bridle), and four pieces ¼" x 1¼" (for the feet). Glue in place as shown in the photograph, adding a strip of braid on the midsection. Cut dots for eyes and triangles for ears from black felt, gluing them as shown. Bend the horse into position.

A HEAVENLY FLIGHT

This demure angel, with her hands folded in prayer, hangs in the center of a cloud of eyelet and is surrounded by stars. She looks lovely in a window but may also be hung over a baby's crib. Or suspend the mobile above a Christmas tree as a novel tree topper. The angel requires only simple sewing, a touch of embroidery, and a little machine or hand quilting on the wings.

YOU WILL NEED:
patterns on page 151
scrap of dotted Swiss or mini print
¼ yd. white eyelet fabric
2½" strip (45" wide) white cotton
6" (1½"-wide) double-edged eyelet trim
9" (2½"-wide) gathered eyelet trim (dress)
⅜ yd. polyester batting
yarn for hair
embroidery floss (light brown and pink)
½ yd. (½"-wide) gathered eyelet trim
1½ yds. (¼"-wide) lace edging
1 yd. (1"-wide) gathered eyelet trim
6" plastic ring
crochet cotton twine for hanging mobile

ANGEL: Cut 2 angel bodies from dotted Swiss, 8 stars and 2 wings from white eyelet, and 1 face appliqué from white cotton. Stitch a strip of ungathered 1½"-wide eyelet down the center of the front body piece. Stitch a 4" piece of 2½"-wide gathered eyelet to the hem of the dress, with right sides together. Press seam towards dress.

Fold under the ¼"-wide seam allowance on the face shape; then appliqué the face to the front of the body with blind stitch. Sew the two body pieces, right sides together, with ¼" seam allowance, leaving the bottom of the skirt open. Clip at curves and turn right side out. Fill the angel with polyester stuffing, using a pencil to push stuffing into the arms. Slip stitch the opening closed, leaving the ruffle hanging below the skirt.

Cut 5 or 6 strands of yarn about 11" long. Secure the center of each at the top of the angel's face; then tack again at ear level on each side. Loop ends of yarn to the back of the head and tack in place at the neck. Embroider the face with two strands of floss, using brown straight stitch for the eyelashes and pink satin stitch for the mouth.

Cut one wing pattern *without any seam allowance* from polyester batting. Baste a narrow strip of gathered eyelet edging all around the right side of one of the eyelet wing pieces, aligning the gathered edge with the raw edges of the wing piece. Right sides together, stitch the two wing pieces around the outside "U," leaving the inside "U" at the top of the wing open. Turn the wing right side out and insert the polyester batting. Slip stitch the opening. Quilt through all three layers by hand or machine along lines indicated on the pattern. Tack the wings to the back of the angel at the points designated as "X" on the pattern.

STARS: Cut 4 stars from polyester batting. Each of the finished stars consists of two star pieces cut from eyelet fabric and one cut from batting. Sandwich the polyester between the two eyelet stars, with the right sides of both eyelet pieces to the outside. Stitch around all sides of the star, close to the edge. Go back and overcast the edges with a machine zigzag stitch or by hand. Trim with narrow lace around the edge of the stars to cover the stitching.

HALO: To make the halo, cut a strip of white cotton 2½" wide and one yard long. Sew gathered eyelet trim to one edge with a narrow seam and sew the ends of the strip together to form a circle. Fold the circle over the ring, turning under the white fabric to meet the eyelet edge. Slip stitch the fabrics together around the ring, easing fullness as you go along, and letting the eyelet extend over the outside edge.

ASSEMBLY: Cut two 15"-long pieces of crochet cotton twine. Attach the two ends of each string to covered ring at exactly opposite points. The ring is divided into quarters by the two strings.

Attach one end of another 15" piece of twine to the angel, above the wings on the back. Tie the loose end of the twine to the two pieces already on the ring, at the point where those two pieces intersect. Leave a piece of the angel's twine long enough to tie a loop at the top for hanging. Put a small dab of glue over the knot to secure. Attach a piece of twine (about 12" long) to each of the stars. Sew loose ends of the twine to the ring, evenly spacing the 4 hanging stars.

OLD-TIMEY GAMEBOARD

Invite Dad to pull up a chair and join in a game of checkers on a gameboard you've made yourself. Although the gameboard is new, it has the well-worn look that usually comes only with age. It is not age but the very careful antiquing process applied to the finished gameboard that gives it such an authentic appearance. Make the gameboard, and some checkers cut from a dowel, for a gift that fits right in with the comfortable "country look."

YOU WILL NEED:
6 feet (½" x 12") pine lumber
3 feet of parting stop (a type of molding available at lumberyards)
table saw or circular saw
handsaw and hammer
small finishing nails
woodworker's glue
semi-gloss latex paint
small and medium-sized artist's brushes
medium-grit sandpaper
antique brown oil-based stain
12" (1"-diameter) dowel

The wood specified is not a standard thickness, although lumberyards in larger cities often carry thinner than usual lumber for special uses. If you cannot find wood of this thickness, do not substitute plywood. Instead, buy standard 1"-thick lumber, take it to a cabinet shop, and have it planed down to a ½" thickness.

Rip two pieces (1¼"-wide) down the entire length of the 6-foot-long piece of 12" pine, using either a table saw or a circular saw. Set these pieces aside.

Rip the length of the board again, this time dividing the board into two pieces approximately 4"-wide and 4¾"-wide. From each of these lengths, cut two pieces 28" long. You should have two pieces 28" x 4" and two pieces 28" x 4¾".

Cut two (17½"-long) strips of parting stop. Arrange the four (28"-long) pieces side by

side so that ends are even. Let there be a slight (no more than 1/16"-wide) gap between each piece. Four inches from each end, draw a line across all 4 pieces. Nail the two strips of parting stop along these two lines, first nailing several nails from the top, then several from the bottom.

From the two 6-foot-long pieces that you set aside, cut lengths of wood to make a frame: two pieces 28"-long and two pieces the exact width of your gameboard. (These pieces should be cut with 45° mitered corners like a picture frame.) Run a line of glue along the side of each strip at the bottom and nail in place to form a frame. Wipe off excess glue and allow to dry.

Paint the entire board with barn red latex paint. Draw a 2" grid in the middle, centering the design; there should be eight 2" squares each way. Paint alternate squares with cream-colored paint. Paint a narrow border around the grid and a small square at each corner with black paint. Using this same black, paint two thin lines across the width of the gameboard at each end (see photograph). After this color dries, paint a small cream-colored star in each square. Allow paint to dry.

Sand all surfaces of the gameboard, including the back, so that some bare wood shows through. Sand particularly well on the corners, the top of the frame, and other points where wear and tear would have occurred through the years.

Use a hammer to make dents at the corners and in a few other places. Use a nail to make several scratches on the surface—don't overdo this step.

Apply a coat of stain to the entire gameboard. Wipe off with a rag, leaving a little bit in the corners. This will give a mellow look to the wood which makes it hard to distinguish from a real antique.

Cut 24 checkers (approximately ¼"-thick) from the dowel with a handsaw. Dip half of these in brown stain and leave the other half natural wood.

ORNAMENTAL EGGS

Egg-fanciers will enjoy making these ornaments from hollow goose eggs—and their children will be wide-eyed with amazement when they compare the size of the ornaments to the more familiar hen's eggs. Small pictures cut from gift wrap or cards decorate each side, and honey-colored shellac gives the eggs an "old world" finish.

YOU WILL NEED:
goose eggs
gold spray paint (optional)
gift wrap or cards
white household glue
orange shellac
thin gold thread
velvet cord

Obtain goose eggs from shops selling eggery supplies or perhaps from a farmer's market. Hollow them out, if necessary, by breaking a ¼"-wide hole in the large end with a corsage pin and shaking out the blended contents. To make the lighter ornament, leave the egg its natural color; for the darker one, spray with gold paint. Cut small motifs from gift wrap, and clip at ¼" intervals around the edges to make the paper conform to the shape of the egg. Brush a thin coat of glue on the back of each cutout, and smooth the paper onto the egg. Allow it to dry.

Brush on one coat of orange shellac to give an "antique" finish. To avoid damaging the shellac, dry the egg upside down on a length of coat hanger wire stuck into a piece of plastic foam. When dry, make a loop for hanging from thin gold thread, gluing it in place. Trim with a bow of velvet cord.

HOLD STILL FOR A KISS

How many times have you lingered under a kissing ball—hoping that someone special would see you standing there and come over to give you a great big Christmas kiss? Continue this lovely Victorian tradition in your family by hanging a kissing ball of natural greenery from a chandelier, over a door, or at the window.

The foliage will last a surprisingly long time because of the way the ball is constructed with a potato as the base. Choose a large, firm potato; then push a loop of strong but flexible wire (a wire coat hanger perhaps) through the bottom of the potato in two places. Twist the ends of the wire together at the top.

Many varieties of fine-textured greenery work well in a kissing ball. Some, such as boxwood, have stems stiff enough to push directly into the base. Others, such as the cedar shown here, require extra support. Wire several sprigs together on a floral pick to form a full bunch and insert the pick into the base.

Cover the potato completely with greenery, forming a full ball. To maintain the round shape, trim any sprigs that are uneven. Decorate the top of the ball with nuts, pine cones, or berries wired to a floral pick. Wrap the wire loop at the top with ribbon, leaving a long strip for hanging. Finish with a fluffy bow.

TARTAN ANGEL

There are so many people you'd like to remember with a small gift at Christmas—a favorite teacher, the choir director, or perhaps the neighbor who has taken special interest in your child. This year give each of them a jaunty plaid angel to serve as a handmade reminder of your friendship and appreciation.

Because she is made from pleated ribbon, a bead, and a pipe cleaner, this little angel ornament is inexpensive as well as quick to complete. Give one to hang on the tree or several to tuck into greenery as a mantel decoration.

YOU WILL NEED:
wooden bead for head (may be purchased with painted features)
acrylic paint (optional)
24" (3"-wide) ribbon with non-woven edges
½ gold pipe cleaner
yellow spun fur
10" (⅛"-wide) satin ribbon
white household glue
very thin wire

Paint eyes and a mouth on the bead if it does not already have facial features painted on it. Allow to dry.

From the 3"-wide ribbon, cut one strip 12" long (for body) and two strips 6" long (for wings). Pleat in an accordion fashion, with pleats no more than ½" wide.

Bend one end of the pipe cleaner into a loop for a halo. Run the straight end down through the head, gluing a tiny bit of yellow fur at the base of the halo to hide the hole. Place the pleated body on top of the pipe cleaner. Connect by wrapping several times with wire, about ½" under the head. Place one pleated wing on each side and continue wrapping tightly several more times. The middle of each wing will be at the same level as the wire wrapped around the body (see photograph). Add a bow of narrow satin ribbon to hide the wire.

COOK UP A GIFT

HOT MUSTARD SAUCE
MUSHROOM MERINGUES
ORANGE BUTTER
ORANGE-NUT BREAD
PARTY CHEESE BALLS
PARMESAN BREADSTICKS
COFFEE LIQUEUR
CUMIN CASHEWS
CRANBERRY-WINE JELLY
FAVORITE POPCORN BALLS
CHOCOLATE-PEANUT BUTTER SAUCE
CURRIED MAYONNAISE
ALL-NATURAL GRANOLA

The very mention of the word "Christmas" makes many people head for the kitchen—to mix, fix, knead, and sometimes even nibble a variety of tasty goodies to give as presents. This is the time to whip up a batch of the dip that your neighbor always loves or of the bread your favorite uncle enjoyed so much that he asked for seconds. And the gift is doubled if you include the recipe when you present the food.

Think of the foods that your friends would really appreciate. Are they entertaining frequently over the holidays? Then give them Party Cheese Balls, piquant Hot Mustard Sauce, or mouth-watering Mushroom Meringues. Do they have small children at home? Then they would undoubtedly like All-Natural Granola or the Chocolate-Peanut Butter Sauce for ice cream. (And their kids would be thrilled to receive a chewy old-fashioned Popcorn Ball!)

For your friend's Christmas breakfast, there's a delicate Orange Butter to spread on warm Orange-Nut Bread. For dinners by the fire, there are crisp Parmesan Breadsticks and a spicy Curried Mayonnaise.

Some of the recipes, like Cranberry-Wine Jelly and Coffee Liqueur, may be made months ahead. Others, such as the breadsticks and the Orange-Nut Bread, are best when prepared just before you need them.

HOT MUSTARD SAUCE
1 cup dry mustard
1 cup tarragon vinegar
3 eggs, beaten
1 cup sugar

Combine mustard and vinegar; mix well, and let stand overnight.

Combine mustard mixture, eggs, and sugar in top of a double boiler. Cook over boiling water, stirring constantly, until slightly thickened. Chill. (Mixture thickens when chilled.) Serve as a sauce for cocktail sausages or ham chunks. Yield: 2¼ cups.

MUSHROOM MERINGUES
3 egg whites
¼ teaspoon cream of tartar
½ cup sugar
⅓ cup semisweet chocolate morsels
Cocoa

Beat egg whites (at room temperature) and cream of tartar until soft peaks form. Gradually add sugar, 1 tablespoon at a time, beating until stiff peaks form. Spoon meringue into a decorating bag fitted with metal tip No. 12.

Line a baking sheet with parchment paper. Pipe equal amounts of mushroom caps and stems onto parchment paper. (To make caps, pipe mounds of meringue about 1¼ inches in diameter; smooth tops with a metal spatula. To make stems, pipe strips about 1½ inches long and ¾ inch in diameter; smooth any peaks with spatula.) Bake at 225° for 1 hour or until thoroughly dry. Cool, then gently peel from paper. Using a sharp knife, cut a small hole in bottom of mushroom caps for stems to fit into.

Melt chocolate morsels in top of double boiler. Spread chocolate over bottoms of

Tempting gifts of food will please everyone on your list. Clockwise from top: Hot Mustard Sauce, Mushroom Meringues, Orange Butter, Orange-Nut Bread, Party Cheese Balls, Cranberry-Wine Jelly, Parmesan Breadsticks, and Coffee Liqueur.

These cleverly-disguised meringues look exactly like mushrooms but taste more like cookies!

mushroom caps, using a small metal spatula. Insert a stem into each mushroom cap. Turn cap-side-down until chocolate hardens. When hardened, turn mushrooms right-side-up and lightly sift with cocoa. Store in air-tight container. Yield: about 3 dozen.

ORANGE BUTTER
1 cup butter
2 tablespoons powdered sugar
Grated rind of 1 lemon
Grated rind of 1 orange
Juice of 1 orange

Combine all ingredients; beat with an electric mixer until orange juice is absorbed. Store in refrigerator. Use as a spread on bread, biscuits, muffins or pancakes. Yield: 2 cups.

Special containers can add to the gift—choose interesting antique dishes, printed tins, Lucite® boxes, baskets, or even holiday napkins as "wraps" for your recipes.

ORANGE-NUT BREAD
¾ cup orange juice
1 cup sugar
½ cup raisins
½ cup coarsely chopped walnuts or pecans
1 egg, slightly beaten
2 tablespoons grated orange rind
2 tablespoons butter or margarine
1¾ cups all-purpose flour
1 teaspoon baking powder
½ teaspoon baking soda
½ teaspoon salt
1 cup sifted powdered sugar
1½ tablespoons water

Combine first 7 ingredients, mixing well. Stir together next 4 ingredients. Add nut mixture to flour mixture, and stir well.

Pour batter evenly into two greased and floured 7- x 3- x 2-inch loafpans. Bake at 350° for 30 to 35 minutes. Cool in pans 5 minutes; turn out onto a wire rack.

Combine sugar and water, stirring well. Drizzle glaze over loaves. Yield: 2 loaves.

PARTY CHEESE BALLS

2 (8-ounce) packages cream cheese, softened
1 (8-ounce) package sharp Cheddar cheese, shredded
1 tablespoon chopped pimiento
1 tablespoon chopped green pepper
1 tablespoon finely chopped onion
2 tablespoons Worcestershire sauce
1 teaspoon lemon juice
Dash of red pepper
Dash of salt
Finely chopped walnuts
Chopped fresh parsley
Paprika

Combine cream cheese and Cheddar cheese, blending well. Stir in the next 7 ingredients. Shape into 3 balls; roll 1 in chopped walnuts, 1 in chopped parsley, and 1 in paprika. Chill. Serve at room temperature. Yield: 3 cheese balls.

PARMESAN BREADSTICKS

1 package dry yeast
⅔ cup warm water (105° to 115°)
2 to 2½ cups all-purpose flour
2 teaspoons sugar
¾ teaspoon salt
¼ cup vegetable oil
1 egg white
1 tablespoon water
2 tablespoons grated Parmesan cheese

Dissolve yeast in ⅔ cup warm water in a large mixing bowl. Stir in 1 cup flour, sugar, salt, and oil; beat until smooth. Stir in enough remaining flour to make soft dough.

Turn dough out onto a floured surface, and knead about 5 minutes until smooth and elastic. Divide dough into 30 equal pieces. Roll each piece into a strip about 6 inches long. Place strips, 1-inch apart, on greased baking sheets. Cover and let rise in a warm place (85°), free from drafts, 30 minutes or until doubled in bulk.

Beat egg white and 1 tablespoon water until frothy. Lightly brush egg white mixture over breadsticks, and sprinkle with Parmesan cheese. Bake at 350° for 20 minutes or until golden brown. Yield: 2½ dozen.

COFFEE LIQUEUR

3 cups sugar
3 cups water
3½ tablespoons instant coffee granules
1 quart vodka
1 tablespoon vanilla extract

Combine sugar, water, and coffee granules in a heavy saucepan. Bring to a boil; cover and simmer for 1 hour. Remove from heat and cool. Stir in vodka and vanilla; pour into bottles and cover with plastic wrap. Punch holes in plastic wrap and store in a dark place for 4 weeks. For later use, store in airtight containers. Yield: about 2 quarts.

CUMIN CASHEWS

2 cups raw cashews
2 tablespoons butter or margarine, melted
1 tablespoon vegetable oil
½ teaspoon salt
½ teaspoon paprika
¼ teaspoon ground cumin seeds

Combine cashews, butter, and oil; spread cashew mixture evenly in a 15- x 10- x 1-inch jellyroll pan. Bake at 350° for 20 minutes, shaking frequently. Drain cashews on paper towels.

Combine salt, paprika, and cumin seeds; sprinkle over cashews. Yield: 2 cups.

CRANBERRY-WINE JELLY

3 cups sugar
1 cup cranberry juice cocktail
1 cup Burgundy or other dry, red wine
1 (3-ounce) package liquid fruit pectin

Combine sugar, cranberry juice cocktail, and wine in a Dutch oven; bring to a rolling boil. Cook 1 minute, stirring frequently. Add fruit pectin; cook, stirring constantly until mixture returns to a boil. Continue boiling 1 minute, stirring frequently. Remove from heat, and skim off foam with a metal spoon.

Quickly pour jelly into hot sterilized jars, leaving ¼-inch headspace. Cover at once with metal lids, and screw bands tight. Process in boiling water bath 5 minutes. Yield: 4 half-pints.

FAVORITE POPCORN BALLS
4 cups sugar
1½ cups light corn syrup
1½ cups water
1 tablespoon salt
1 cup butter or margarine
2 teaspoons vanilla extract
6 quarts popped corn

Combine sugar, corn syrup, water, and salt in a saucepan; cook over medium heat, stirring until sugar dissolves. Cook, without stirring, until syrup reaches a hard ball stage on a candy thermometer (250°). Remove from heat, and stir in butter and vanilla.

Place popped corn in a large pan; pour hot syrup over top, mixing well. Grease hands with butter, and shape mixture into balls; place on waxed paper to dry. Yield: about 2 dozen.

CHOCOLATE-PEANUT BUTTER SAUCE
1 (6-ounce) package semisweet chocolate morsels
¼ cup crunchy peanut butter
¼ cup light corn syrup
¼ cup plus 1 tablespoon whipping cream

Melt chocolate morsels in top of a double boiler. Add peanut butter, stirring until well blended. Remove from heat, and stir in corn syrup and whipping cream. Serve warm over ice cream. Yield: about 1¼ cups.

Note: Store in refrigerator. Reheat over low heat before using. If sauce becomes too thick, stir in a small amount of whipping cream.

CURRIED MAYONNAISE
2 cups mayonnaise
2 teaspoons curry powder
2 teaspoons lemon juice
2 teaspoons grated onion
2 teaspoons sweet pickle juice

Combine all ingredients, mixing well. Chill. Serve with assorted fresh vegetables. Yield: 2 cups.

ALL-NATURAL GRANOLA
½ cup safflower oil
½ cup honey
½ teaspoon vanilla extract
4 cups regular oats, uncooked
1 cup wheat germ
1 cup sliced almonds
1 cup sunflower seeds
½ cup sesame seeds
½ cup bran cereal
1 cup raisins (optional)

Combine oil, honey, and vanilla; blend well, and set aside. Combine remaining ingredients except raisins in a large bowl; add oil mixture, mixing well.

Spread granola on a large baking sheet; bake at 250° for 45 minutes, stirring every 15 minutes. Stir in raisins, if desired. Store in airtight containers. Yield: about 12 cups.

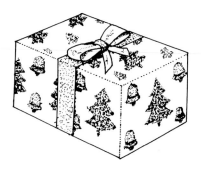

Clockwise from the top left, the cookies are: Mint Meringue Cookies, Peppermint Spirals, Gingerbread Men, Red Raspberry Cookies, Toasted Almond Fingers, Decorated Sugar Cookies, and Cherry Bonbons.

NEIGHBORHOOD COOKIE SWAP

GINGERBREAD MEN
(WITH ROYAL ICING)
CHERRY BONBONS
RED RASPBERRY COOKIES
DELICATE LEMON SQUARES

MINT MERINGUE COOKIES
PEPPERMINT SPIRALS
TOASTED ALMOND FINGERS
DECORATED SUGAR COOKIES
CHOCOLATE MINT LAYER COOKIES

Each guest can pack a basket with her own favorite cookies, as well as the recipes.

Half the fun of Christmas is visiting and renewing friendships, especially with good neighbors that you'd like to see more often. And who ever has enough cookies on hand during the holidays? Though you may begin with enough to offer friends, there always seem to be little hands dipping into the cookie jar.

This year, join forces with your neighbors by baking cookies to share with each other and have a delightful party in the process. Each friend will have her family specialties— and this will be a wonderful opportunity to sample a wide variety of goodies that you've never made yourself. The recipes given here are so tasty that they are likely to become your own family's new favorites.

Bake a dozen cookies for each friend attending the party—plus some to nibble. Then make copies of the recipe to go along with them. As each person arrives, she adds her cookies to those already there. Serve coffee or tea, and let each guest nibble until the time comes for her to take a new assortment of cookies home to her family.

While the original container may be used to hold the treats, you might choose to furnish frilly holiday gift sacks lined with tissue paper or even colorful painted baskets lined with napkins. Regardless of how the cookies are packed, your neighbors will leave with a warm feeling in their hearts and probably with the desire to make the cookie swap an annual event.

GINGERBREAD MEN

½ cup butter or margarine, softened
¾ cup sugar
1 egg, beaten
¼ cup molasses
Juice of ½ orange
3½ to 4 cups all-purpose flour
½ teaspoon salt
1 teaspoon baking soda
1 teaspoon ground cinnamon
1 teaspoon ground ginger
Raisins
Royal Icing

Cream butter and sugar until light and fluffy; beat in egg, molasses, and orange juice. Combine dry ingredients, and blend into creamed mixture. Chill dough about one hour or until stiff enough to handle.

Work with half of dough at a time; store remainder in refrigerator. Roll dough to ¼- to ⅛-inch thickness on greased cookie sheets. Cut with a 2- or 5-inch gingerbread man cutter, and remove excess dough. Press several raisins into dough for eyes, noses, and buttons.

Bake at 350° for 10 minutes. Cool 1 minute; remove cookies to rack to complete cooling. Decorate as desired with Royal Icing. Yield: about 3 dozen (5-inch) or 9 dozen (2-inch) cookies.

ROYAL ICING

3 large egg whites
½ teaspoon cream of tartar
1 (16-ounce) package powdered sugar
Paste food coloring (optional)

Combine egg whites and cream of tartar in a large mixing bowl. Beat at medium speed with an electric mixer until frothy. Gradually add powdered sugar, mixing well. Beat for 5 to 7 minutes. Stir in paste food coloring, if desired. Yield: about 2 cups.

Note: Icing dries very quickly; keep covered at all times with plastic wrap. Do not double this recipe. If additional icing is needed, make two batches.

CHERRY BONBONS

1½ cups sifted powdered sugar
1 cup butter or margarine, softened
1½ tablespoons vanilla extract
2¾ cups all-purpose flour
¼ teaspoon salt
1 tablespoon milk
2 (8-ounce) jars maraschino cherries, drained
Rainbow Glaze (recipe follows)
Chocolate Glaze (recipe follows)
Chopped walnuts

Combine sugar, butter, and vanilla, mixing well; stir in flour, salt, and milk. For each cookie, shape 1 tablespoon dough around a cherry; place cookies 1-inch apart on ungreased cookie sheets. Bake at 350° for 12 to 15 minutes. Cool cookies on wire racks.

Dip tops of cookies in rainbow glaze or chocolate glaze; sprinkle immediately with chopped walnuts. Yield: about 3 dozen.

Rainbow Glaze:

2½ cups sifted powdered sugar
3 to 4 tablespoons water
Yellow, pink, and green food coloring

Combine sugar and water; beat until smooth. Divide glaze into 3 equal portions; make yellow, pink, and green glaze by stirring in a few drops of food coloring. Yield: about 1 cup.

Chocolate Glaze:

1 cup sifted powdered sugar
2 to 3 tablespoons water
1 (1-ounce) square unsweetened chocolate, melted
1 teaspoon vanilla extract

Combine all ingredients; beat until smooth. Yield: about ½ cup.

RED RASPBERRY COOKIES

2 cups butter or margarine, softened
½ cup sugar
2 teaspoons almond extract
1 teaspoon salt
4 cups all-purpose flour
Sesame seeds
Raspberry preserves

Cream butter and sugar until light and fluffy. Add almond extract, salt, and flour, mixing well. Wrap dough tightly in plastic wrap and chill for 1 hour. Shape dough into 1-inch balls, and roll in sesame seeds. Place on lightly greased baking sheets. Flatten cookies slightly, and indent centers with thumb; fill with raspberry preserves. Bake at 400° for 12 to 15 minutes. Remove to wire racks to cool. Yield: about 5 dozen.

DELICATE LEMON SQUARES

1 cup all-purpose flour
¼ cup sifted powdered sugar
½ cup butter or margarine
2 tablespoons all-purpose flour
½ teaspoon baking powder
2 eggs, beaten
1 cup sugar
½ teaspoon grated lemon rind
3 tablespoons lemon juice
2 tablespoons powdered sugar

Mix 1 cup flour and ¼ cup powdered sugar; cut in butter with pastry blender until mixture resembles coarse meal. Press mixture evenly into a 9-inch square baking pan. Bake at 350° for 15 minutes.

Combine 2 tablespoons flour and baking powder; set aside. Combine eggs, sugar, lemon rind, and lemon juice; beat well. Stir dry ingredients into egg mixture, and pour over baked crust. Bake at 350° for 20 minutes or until lightly browned and set. Sprinkle lightly with 2 tablespoons powdered sugar. Let cool, and cut into squares. Yield: about 3 dozen.

MINT MERINGUE COOKIES

2 egg whites
½ teaspoon mint and peppermint extract
½ cup sugar
6 drops green food coloring (optional)
1 (6-ounce) package semisweet chocolate morsels

Combine egg whites (at room temperature) and mint extract; beat until frothy. Gradually add sugar, 1 tablespoon at a time, beating until the egg whites are glossy and stiff peaks form. Beat in food coloring, if desired. Do not underbeat.

Fold chocolate morsels into meringue. Drop meringue by rounded teaspoonfuls onto buttered cookie sheets. Bake at 200° for 1 hour or until dry and set. Cookies should not brown. Transfer to wire racks to cool. Yield: about 2½ dozen.

PEPPERMINT SPIRALS

1 cup butter or margarine, softened
1½ cups sugar
1 egg
1 teaspoon peppermint extract
2½ cups all-purpose flour
1½ teaspoons baking powder
½ teaspoon salt
Red food coloring

Cream butter; gradually add sugar, beating until light and fluffy. Add egg and peppermint extract; beat well. Combine flour, baking powder, and salt; add this to creamed mixture, beating just until blended.

Divide dough in half; add a few drops red food coloring to one half, and knead until coloring is evenly distributed. Cover and refrigerate both halves until firm. On floured waxed paper, roll each half of dough to a 16-x 8-inch rectangle. Invert white dough onto red dough; peel waxed paper from white dough. Tightly roll dough in jellyroll fashion, starting at long end, and peeling waxed paper from red dough as you roll. Cover and refrigerate several hours. Slice dough ¼-inch thick and place on ungreased cookie sheets. Bake at 350° for 10 to 12 minutes. Remove to wire racks to cool. Yield: about 5 dozen.

TOASTED ALMOND FINGERS
1 cup butter or margarine, softened
¾ cup sifted powdered sugar
1 tablespoon milk
1 teaspoon vanilla extract
2 cups all-purpose flour
¼ teaspoon salt
2 cups finely chopped, toasted almonds
1 (6-ounce) package semisweet chocolate morsels
1 tablespoon shortening

Cream butter and sugar until light and fluffy. Beat in milk and vanilla; add flour and salt, and mix well. Stir in almonds. Chill dough thoroughly.

Shape dough into 2-inch "fingers," using 1 tablespoon dough for each; place on ungreased cookie sheets. Bake at 325° for 15 to 17 minutes or until lightly browned. Cool.

Melt chocolate and shortening in top of double boiler over hot water. Dip one end of each finger in chocolate, letting excess drip off; place cookies on wire racks until chocolate is firm. Yield: about 4 dozen.

DECORATED SUGAR COOKIES
½ cup butter or margarine, softened
¾ cup sugar
¾ teaspoon vanilla extract
1 egg
2 cups all-purpose flour
½ teaspoon baking soda
½ teaspoon salt
Royal Icing (recipe on page 95)

Cream butter and sugar until light and fluffy; add vanilla and egg, mixing well. Combine flour, soda, and salt; add to creamed mixture, blending well (mixture will be very stiff).

Divide dough into 3 parts; roll each part on lightly floured waxed paper to ⅛-inch thickness.

Cut dough with desired cutters, and place on lightly greased cookie sheets. Bake at 375° for 8 to 10 minutes or until lightly browned. Let cool on wire racks. Spoon colored Royal Icing into decorating bags. Pipe outlines on cookies using metal tip No. 3. Fill in between outlines by piping connecting stars, using metal tip No. 16 or 18. Let dry. Yield: about 5 dozen (2½-inch) cookies.

CHOCOLATE MINT LAYER COOKIES
2 (1-ounce) squares unsweetened chocolate
½ cup butter or margarine
2 eggs
1 cup sugar
½ cup all-purpose flour
½ cup chopped walnuts or pecans
1½ cups powdered sugar
3 tablespoons butter or margarine, softened
2 tablespoons whipping cream
¾ teaspoon mint and peppermint extract
1 to 2 drops green food coloring
½ (4-ounce) package sweet baking chocolate
2 tablespoons butter or margarine
1 teaspoon vanilla extract

Melt unsweetened chocolate and ½ cup butter in top of a double boiler; cool. Beat eggs and 1 cup sugar until light and thick; stir in flour, walnuts, and melted chocolate. Spoon mixture into a greased 9-inch square baking pan, spreading evenly. Bake at 350° for 25 minutes; cool in pan on a wire rack.

Combine powdered sugar, 3 tablespoons butter, whipping cream, mint extract, and food coloring, if desired; beat until smooth. Spread evenly over baked layer; cover and chill 1 hour or until firm.

Melt sweet chocolate and 2 tablespoons butter in top of a double boiler; stir in vanilla, and drizzle over mint layer. Cover and chill 1 hour or until firm. Cut into 1-inch squares. Yield: about 7 dozen.

OPEN HOUSE FOR A CROWD

(FOR 15 TO 20 PEOPLE)

CHICKEN LIVER PÂTÉ   CRACKERS
OPEN-FACED MINI REUBENS
AVOCADO DIP   FRESH VEGETABLES
HONEY-BUTTER CHICKEN TIDBITS
HOT SPINACH DIP   TACO CHIPS
SPICED ALMONDS
SAUSAGE-CHEDDAR NUGGETS
SNOWFLAKE CREAM PUFFS
NUTTY CRANBERRY LOAVES
CRANBERRY PARTY PUNCH

Invite all those friends you've enjoyed seeing throughout the year to share in an evening of fun and fellowship, with plenty of good food on the table! The convivial atmosphere of an open house, with friends and neighbors jostling elbows, is a wonderful way to break the ice and entertain a number of people at one time. If you stagger the hours on your invitations, many friends may drop by over the course of the evening—and even a small house can hold lots of people this way!

Give your guests a chance to nibble on a variety of healthy, yet not too expensive, snacks—each recipe serves from 15 to 20 people. If you'd like fairly substantial foods, serve the delectable Honey-Butter Chicken Tidbits, Open-Faced Mini Reuben sandwiches, or Sausage-Cheddar Nuggets. On the lighter side, try Hot Spinach Dip, Avocado Dip, or Chicken Liver Pâté with plenty of chips and crackers. Your dieting friends will appreciate your choice of crisp, fresh vegetables beautifully presented on a "Christmas tree" of parsley. And those friends with a sweet tooth will find it hard to stay away from the crunchy Spiced Almonds or the melt-in-your-mouth Snowflake Cream Puffs. These and the other recipes will make a memorable party—one that you might even decide to repeat next year.

CHICKEN LIVER PÂTÉ
1 pound chicken livers
2 tablespoons chopped green onion
2 tablespoons chopped celery
2 tablespoons chopped green pepper
¼ cup butter or margarine
½ cup commercial sour cream
⅓ cup minced blanched almonds
1½ teaspoons anchovy paste
½ teaspoon dried basil leaves
¼ teaspoon freshly ground pepper
Carrot flowers
Green onion stems

Sauté chicken livers, green onion, celery, and green pepper in butter until livers are done. Place the liver mixture, and the next 5 ingredients in the container of a food processor; then process with a metal blade until smooth.

Spoon pâté into a lightly oiled 2-cup mold; chill overnight. Unmold onto serving platter and garnish pâté with carrot flowers and green onion stems. Serve with crackers. Yield: 2 cups.

OPEN-FACED MINI REUBENS
¾ cup Thousand Island dressing
36 slices party rye bread
2¼ cups well-drained chopped sauerkraut
¾ pound thinly sliced corned beef
⅓ pound sliced Swiss cheese

Spread 1 teaspoon dressing on each slice of bread. Place 1 tablespoon sauerkraut on each slice of bread, and top with a slice of corned beef. Cut cheese the size of bread, and place over corned beef.

Arrange sandwiches on a baking sheet; bake at 400° for 10 minutes or until cheese melts. Yield: 3 dozen.

Tasty tidbits include (clockwise from top right): Avocado Dip and fresh vegetables, Nutty Cranberry Loaves, Snowflake Cream Puffs, Chicken Liver Pâté, Open-Faced Mini Reubens, Hot Spinach Dip, Cranberry Party Punch.

AVOCADO DIP

2 medium avocados, peeled
2 tablespoons lime juice
1 tablespoon grated onion
1 teaspoon seasoned salt
¼ teaspoon hot sauce
2 (3-ounce) packages cream cheese, softened
⅓ cup milk

Mash avocados with a fork. Combine avocado, lime juice, onion, salt, and hot sauce; set aside. Beat cream cheese with electric mixer until smooth; gradually add milk, mixing well.

Stir cream cheese mixture into avocado mixture; chill. Yield: about 2½ cups.

Serve with assorted fresh vegetables. If desired, make a green "tree" with sprigs of parsley attached by hairpins to a plastic foam cone. Insert a toothpick into each cut vegetable and arrange on the tree.

HONEY-BUTTER CHICKEN TIDBITS

6 large broiler-fryer chicken thighs, boned
¼ cup butter or margarine, melted
¼ cup honey
1 teaspoon teriyaki sauce
1 teaspoon seasoned salt
¼ teaspoon pepper
⅛ teaspoon garlic powder
½ cup sesame seeds, toasted

Rinse chicken thighs and pat dry. Cut the meat on each thigh into 6 to 8 pieces; then refrigerate 8 hours.

Combine butter, honey, and teriyaki sauce in a small saucepan; stir well. Bring to boil; remove from heat, and set aside.

Sprinkle chicken pieces with seasoned salt, pepper, and garlic powder. Dip chicken pieces into honey mixture, and coat with sesame seeds. Place chicken pieces on a cookie sheet. Bake at 350° for 30 minutes, turning once to brown evenly. Reheat remaining honey mixture, and serve with chicken tidbits. Yield: 3 to 4 dozen.

HOT SPINACH DIP

1 (10-ounce) package frozen chopped spinach
1 (6-ounce) roll process cheese food with garlic, cubed
1 (10¾-ounce) can cream of mushroom soup, undiluted
1 tablespoon Worcestershire sauce
½ teaspoon pepper

Cook spinach according to package directions, omitting salt; drain and press well to remove excess liquid.

Combine cheese and soup in a heavy saucepan; cook over low heat, stirring frequently, until cheese melts. Stir in spinach and remaining ingredients. Serve warm with taco chips. Yield: about 2 cups.

SPICED ALMONDS

1 egg white
1 tablespoon water
2 cups whole unblanched almonds
¾ cup sugar
1 tablespoon pumpkin pie spice
½ teaspoon salt

Combine egg white (at room temperature) and water in a large bowl; beat until frothy. Add almonds and toss until coated.

Combine remaining ingredients and pour over almonds; toss until almonds are well coated. Pour almonds onto lightly greased cookie sheet, spreading into a single layer. Bake at 300° for 25 minutes. Remove immediately to waxed paper; separate into small clusters. Yield: 2 cups.

SAUSAGE-CHEDDAR NUGGETS

1 pound hot bulk sausage
2 cups (8 ounces) shredded sharp Cheddar cheese
2 cups biscuit mix
2 tablespoons grated onion
1 tablespoon poultry seasoning

Combine all ingredients, mixing well. Roll into walnut-size balls. Place on an ungreased baking sheet and bake at 400° for 15 minutes. Drain on absorbent paper towels. Serve hot. Yield: about 4 dozen.

CRANBERRY PARTY PUNCH

3 (12-ounce) cans frozen lemonade concentrate, thawed and diluted
1 quart cranberry juice cocktail
1 cup frozen orange juice concentrate, thawed and undiluted
1 (33.8-ounce) bottle ginger ale, chilled
1 orange, thinly sliced

Combine juices; chill. Add ginger ale just before serving. Garnish with orange slices. Yield: about 1½ gallons.

Note: An extra can of lemonade concentrate may be diluted and frozen to make an ice ring or cubes to use in the punch.

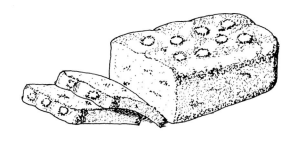

SNOWFLAKE CREAM PUFFS

1 cup water
½ cup butter
1 cup all-purpose flour
4 eggs
1½ cups whipping cream
¼ cup plus 2 tablespoons sifted powdered sugar
Powdered sugar

Combine water and butter in saucepan; bring to a boil. Add flour all at once, stirring

vigorously over low heat for approximately 1 minute or until mixture leaves sides of pan and forms a smooth ball. Remove from heat, and allow to cool slightly.

Add eggs, one at a time, beating with a wooden spoon after each addition; beat until batter is smooth. Pipe mixture into small balls on greased baking sheets using metal decorating tip No. 5B. Bake at 400° for 20 minutes or until golden brown and puffed. Cool away from drafts. Cut top ⅓ off cream puffs; pull out and discard soft dough inside.

Beat whipping cream until foamy; gradually add ¼ cup plus 2 tablespoons powdered sugar, beating until soft peaks form. Fill cream puffs with whipped cream; replace tops of cream puffs. Arrange on platter; sprinkle with powdered sugar. Yield: about 3 dozen.

NUTTY CRANBERRY LOAVES

4 cups all-purpose flour
1¼ cups sugar
2 tablespoons baking powder
1 teaspoon salt
2 cups diced dried apricots
2 cups chopped cranberries
1 cup coarsely chopped walnuts
4 eggs
½ cup milk
½ cup butter or margarine, melted

Combine flour, sugar, baking powder, and salt in a large bowl. Stir in apricots, cranberries, and walnuts, coating well. Make a well in center of mixture.

Beat eggs slightly in a small bowl; stir in milk and butter. Pour into center of flour mixture; stir until all dry ingredients are moistened.

Pour batter into 2 greased 9- x 5- x 3-inch loafpans. Bake at 350° for 50 to 55 minutes or until loaves test done. Let cool in pans 10 minutes. Remove to wire racks, and cool completely. Yield: 2 loaves.

FIRESIDE SUPPER

(10 TO 12 SERVINGS)

MULLED CIDER
SALMON SPREAD   CRACKERS
VEGETABLE-CHEESE SOUP
SPICY BEEF SANDWICH LOAF
MARINATED BROCCOLI
SHERRY-RASPBERRY DREAM
BRAZILIAN COFFEE
HOT BUTTERED RUM
SPICED WALNUTS

Hearts may be warm, but fingers and toes are usually cold after an evening spent caroling from house to house. Invite the whole gang over and serve a deliciously steaming supper in front of the fire.

Begin with hot Mulled Cider and a make-ahead Salmon Spread on crackers, to be enjoyed while the rest of the meal is heating up. Then let each guest help himself to a mug of savory Vegetable-Cheese Soup and a slice of Spicy Beef Sandwich Loaf. Crisp stalks of Marinated Broccoli add just the right accompaniment. And for dessert? A molded Sherry-Raspberry Dream that is sure to delight anyone! Adults in the group might like to linger over a cup of fragrant Brazilian Coffee or Hot Buttered Rum.

MULLED CIDER

3 quarts apple cider
2 cups orange juice
¾ cup firmly packed light brown sugar
1½ teaspoons whole allspice
1½ teaspoons whole cloves
12 (4-inch) cinnamon sticks

Combine apple cider, orange juice, and brown sugar in a large Dutch oven. Tie spices in a cheesecloth bag; drop into cider.

From top right: Salmon Spread, crackers, Vegetable-Cheese Soup, Spicy Beef Sandwich Loaf, Brazilian Coffee, Marinated Broccoli, and Sherry-Raspberry Dream.

Bring to a boil; reduce heat and simmer 15 minutes. Remove bag. Garnish each serving with a cinnamon stick. Yield: 3½ quarts.

SALMON SPREAD

1 (15½-ounce) can red salmon, drained and flaked
1 (8-ounce) package cream cheese, softened
¼ cup minced onion
1 tablespoon lemon juice
1 teaspoon prepared horseradish
¼ teaspoon salt
½ teaspoon liquid smoke

Combine all ingredients; mix well. Chill for at least 2 hours. Serve with crackers. Yield: about 1½ cups.

VEGETABLE-CHEESE SOUP

1 cup butter or margarine, divided
¾ cup finely chopped celery
¾ cup finely chopped carrot
¾ cup finely chopped onion
¾ cup finely chopped green pepper
½ cup plus 1 tablespoon all-purpose flour
6 cups milk
1 (10¾-ounce) can chicken broth, undiluted
3 cups (12 ounces) shredded sharp process American cheese
Chopped fresh parsley

Melt ¼ cup butter in a large skillet; add vegetables, and sauté until crisp-tender. Set vegetables aside.

Melt remaining ¾ cup butter in a large Dutch oven over low heat; add flour, stirring until smooth. Cook 1 minute, stirring constantly. Gradually add milk and cook over medium heat, stirring constantly, until thick and bubbly. Add enough water to chicken broth to make 3 cups. Add chicken broth, cheese, and sautéed vegetables; simmer, stirring frequently, until cheese melts and mixture is well heated (do not boil). Garnish with chopped parsley. Yield: 11 cups.

SPICY BEEF SANDWICH LOAF

2 pounds ground beef
2 small onions, chopped
½ cup chopped green pepper
½ cup chopped celery
2 (8-ounce) cans tomato sauce
¾ cup catsup
2 tablespoons Worcestershire sauce
2 teaspoons dry mustard
½ teaspoon salt
¼ teaspoon pepper
2 (16-ounce) loaves French bread
Leaf lettuce

Combine ground beef, onions, green pepper, and celery in a Dutch oven; cook until meat is browned. Drain off pan drippings. Add next 6 ingredients, and bring to a boil. Cover, reduce heat, and simmer 15 to 20 minutes, stirring occasionally.

Slice off top third of bread loaves. Scoop about 1 inch of bread from bottom slices, leaving ½-inch margin on all sides. Place top slices on bottom slices and wrap loaves in foil. Bake at 350° for 20 minutes. Remove from foil. Arrange lettuce on bottom slices of bread; spoon meat mixture over lettuce. Cover with top of bread, and slice each loaf into 6 equal pieces. Yield: 12 servings.

MARINATED BROCCOLI

2 (1-pound) bunches broccoli
1 cup cider vinegar
½ cup vegetable oil
2 tablespoons sugar
1 teaspoon salt
1 teaspoon pepper
¼ teaspoon garlic powder
1 tablespoon chopped pimiento

Trim off large leaves of broccoli and tough ends of lower stalks. Wash broccoli well, and cut into serving-size spears; arrange spears in a single layer in dish.

Combine remaining ingredients in a jar; cover tightly, and shake vigorously. Pour over broccoli. Cover and chill at least 12 hours, stirring occasionally. Remove broccoli from marinade before serving. Yield: 10 to 12 servings.

SHERRY-RASPBERRY DREAM

3 envelopes unflavored gelatin
½ cup cold water
2 cups boiling water
½ cup cream sherry
4 egg yolks
¾ cup sugar
2 cups whipping cream
Raspberry Sauce (recipe follows)

Soften gelatin in cold water; let stand 1 minute. Add boiling water; stir until gelatin dissolves, scraping sides and bottom of bowl occasionally. Let cool. Stir in sherry.

Beat egg yolks until thick and lemon colored. Add sugar; beat well, and stir in gelatin mixture. Chill until consistency of unbeaten egg white. Beat with wire whisk until smooth.

Beat whipping cream until soft peaks form (do not overbeat); fold into gelatin mixture. Spoon into a lightly oiled 6-cup mold, and chill until set.

Unmold onto serving platter; spoon Raspberry Sauce over mold just before serving. Yield: 12 servings.

Raspberry Sauce:

2 (10-ounce) packages frozen raspberries, thawed
1 cup sugar
2 tablespoons plus 1 teaspoon cornstarch

Combine raspberries and sugar in a saucepan; bring to a boil, and boil 5 minutes. Put mixture through a food mill. Combine a small amount of raspberry sauce and cornstarch; stir into remaining sauce. Cook over low heat, stirring constantly, until smooth and thickened. Cool. Yield: about 2 cups.

BRAZILIAN COFFEE

⅔ cup cocoa
2 teaspoons ground cinnamon
1 teaspoon salt
2 (14-ounce) cans sweetened condensed milk
8 cups water
3 cups strong coffee
Cinnamon sticks
Ground nutmeg

Combine cocoa, cinnamon, and salt in a large Dutch oven. Add sweetened condensed milk, stirring until smooth. Place pan over medium heat; gradually stir in water and coffee. Heat thoroughly (do not boil). Garnish each serving with a cinnamon stick, and sprinkle with nutmeg. Refrigerate leftovers. Yield: 3½ quarts.

Note: Add 1 cup brandy and ½ cup light rum along with water and coffee, if desired.

HOT BUTTERED RUM

1 cup butter or margarine, softened
1 cup firmly packed light brown sugar
2 cups sifted powdered sugar
1½ teaspoons ground cinnamon
1 pint vanilla ice cream, softened
1¾ to 2 cups light rum
7½ cups boiling water
Whipped cream
Ground nutmeg
Cinnamon sticks (optional)

Combine butter, sugar, and cinnamon; beat until light and fluffy. Add ice cream, stirring until well blended. Spoon mixture into a freezer container, and freeze until firm.

To serve, thaw mixture slightly. Combine butter mixture, rum, and boiling water; stir well. Top each serving with whipped cream, and sprinkle with nutmeg. Serve with cinnamon stick stirrers, if desired. Yield: 12 cups.

SPICED WALNUTS

3 tablespoons sugar
2 tablespoons Worcestershire sauce
1½ tablespoons butter or margarine, melted
½ teaspoon salt
⅛ teaspoon garlic powder
⅛ teaspoon hot sauce
3 cups walnut halves

Combine first 6 ingredients in large bowl, mixing well. Add walnuts; stir to coat. Spread mixture evenly in a 13- x 9- x 2-inch baking pan. Bake at 300° for 30 minutes; transfer to waxed paper to cool completely. Yield: 3 cups.

HURRY-HOME MICROWAVE MEAL

(6 SERVINGS)

CHEESY CHICKEN
CHUNKY POTATO SALAD
CRANBERRY-ORANGE RELISH
WILTED SPINACH
HOT STRAWBERRY SUNDAES
TEA   COFFEE

A busy day spent Christmas shopping leaves little time for preparing a nourishing evening meal. Rather than cut short the shopping, short-cut the cooking by relying on your microwave oven and this make-ahead menu. Your family (or friends who come to dinner) will never guess that you raced in at the last minute to add the finishing touches to this delectable dinner.

Before leaving the house, tend to routine preparations like washing the vegetables and setting the table. You may even like to partially prepare the chicken by coating it with crumbs and refrigerating it until you come home. The Chunky Potato Salad and the Cranberry-Orange Relish should be made ahead and allowed to chill.

Call your family to the dining table for a well-balanced and colorful meal of golden Cheesy Chicken, potato salad, Wilted Spinach with bacon, and tangy Cranberry-Orange Relish. If you still have room for dessert, serve ice cream sundaes topped with a hot mixture of strawberry preserves, walnuts and kirsch.

CHEESY CHICKEN
¼ cup plus 2 tablespoons butter or
  margarine
6 chicken breast halves, skinned
3½ cups cheese crackers, crushed

Place butter in a 1-quart glass measure. Microwave at HIGH for 1 minute or until melted. Brush chicken pieces with butter; roll in cracker crumbs. Arrange chicken in a 12- x 8- x 2-inch baking dish or on a microwave-safe meat rack. Cover with waxed paper. Microwave at HIGH for 8 minutes. Rearrange chicken (do not turn) so uncooked portions are to outside of dish. Cover and microwave at HIGH for 8 minutes or until done. Let stand 6 minutes. Yield: 6 servings.

CHUNKY POTATO SALAD
5 medium potatoes, peeled and cut in
  ¾-inch cubes
1 cup water
3 eggs
⅓ cup chopped green onion
⅓ cup chopped celery
⅓ cup shredded carrot
⅓ cup commercial sour cream
1½ tablespoons vinegar
¾ teaspoon dry mustard
½ teaspoon salt
¼ teaspoon pepper
Leaf lettuce (optional)

Combine potatoes and water in a 2-quart casserole; cover with heavy-duty plastic wrap. Microwave at HIGH for 12 to 15 minutes or until tender, stirring after 6 minutes. Drain well, and set aside.

Gently break each egg into a separate 6-ounce custard cup or microwave-safe coffee cup; pierce yolks with a wooden pick. Cover each cup with heavy-duty plastic wrap. Arrange cups in a ring about 2-inches apart in center of microwave oven.

Microwave at MEDIUM (50% power) for 3 to 4 minutes or until eggs are almost set. Test eggs with a wooden pick (yolks should be just firm and whites should be almost set). Let eggs stand, covered, for 1 to 2 minutes to complete cooking. If eggs are not desired degree of doneness after standing, cover and continue microwaving briefly. Let eggs cool. Mash yolks and chop whites.

Dinner includes Wilted Spinach, Chunky Potato Salad, Cranberry-Orange Relish, and Cheesy Chicken.

Combine potatoes, egg whites, green onion, celery, and carrot; mix well. Combine egg yolks, sour cream, vinegar, and seasonings; mix well, and stir into potato mixture. Chill at least 2 hours. Serve in a lettuce-lined bowl. Yield: 6 servings.

CRANBERRY-ORANGE RELISH
2 cups fresh cranberries
1 orange, peeled, seeded, and sectioned
½ cup sugar
¼ cup raisins
¼ cup chopped walnuts
1 tablespoon vinegar
1 tablespoon orange juice
⅛ teaspoon ground ginger

Combine all ingredients in a 2-quart casserole, mixing well. Cover with waxed paper. Microwave at HIGH for 5 to 6 minutes or until berries burst and the liquid is slightly thickened, stirring mixture halfway through cooking. Chill. Yield: about 2 cups.

WILTED SPINACH
3 eggs
6 slices bacon
½ cup sliced green onion
⅓ cup red wine vinegar
1½ tablespoons sugar
1½ tablespoons water
¼ teaspoon salt
About 8 cups fresh spinach, torn

Gently break each egg into a separate 6-ounce custard cup or microwave-safe coffee cup; pierce yolks with a wooden pick. Cover each cup with heavy-duty plastic wrap. Arrange cups in a ring about 2 inches apart in center of microwave oven.

Microwave at MEDIUM (50% power) for 3 to 4 minutes or until eggs are almost set. Test eggs with a wooden pick (yolks should be just firm and whites should be almost set). Let eggs stand, covered, for 1 to 2 minutes

to complete cooking. If eggs are not desired degree of doneness after standing, cover and continue microwaving briefly. Let eggs cool, chop finely, and set aside.

Place bacon on a rack in a 12- x 8- x 2-inch baking dish; cover with paper towels. Microwave at HIGH for 5 to 6 minutes or until crisp. Remove bacon, reserving drippings in dish. Crumble bacon, and set aside.

Add onion to bacon drippings, and cover with waxed paper. Microwave at HIGH for 4 minutes. Add vinegar, sugar, water, and salt. Microwave at HIGH for 3 minutes or until mixture is boiling.

Place spinach in a large bowl. Pour hot dressing over spinach. Add crumbled bacon and chopped egg; toss lightly, and serve immediately. Yield: 6 servings.

HOT STRAWBERRY SUNDAES
Vanilla ice cream
1¼ cups strawberry preserves
¼ cup coarsely chopped walnuts
3 tablespoons kirsch or cherry-flavored brandy

Spoon ice cream into 6 individual serving dishes; place in freezer while cooking strawberry mixture.

Combine strawberry preserves, walnuts, and kirsch in a small microwave-safe bowl. Microwave at MEDIUM (50% power) for 3 to 4 minutes or until the preserves are heated and partially melted. Spoon sauce over ice cream, and serve immediately. Yield: 6 servings.

Clockwise from right: Cheese Biscuits, Creamy Potato Casserole, Hot Gingered Fruit, Sausage-Cheese Bake, Cranberry Coffee Cake.

CHRISTMAS MORNING BRUNCH
(8 TO 10 SERVINGS)

CRANBERRY COFFEE CAKE   *SAUSAGE-CHEESE BAKE*
SUNSHINE BREAKFAST DRINK   *HOT GINGERED FRUIT*
CREAMY POTATO CASSEROLE   *CHEESE BISCUITS*

It's Christmas morning . . . the stockings have been emptied and all the gaily wrapped presents have been opened to the sound of happy squeals. Now—what can you serve that is tasty, yet easy to prepare?

This menu for a mid-morning brunch is hearty enough to please the hungriest grandpa and festive enough to suit the occasion. Best of all, most of the dishes may be made the day before and simply popped into the oven to cook while you enjoy being with your family. (Add a little extra time to the baking required for the recipe if the dish has been refrigerated.)

When the family comes to eat, they'll be treated to a tummy-filling brunch of Sausage-Cheese Bake with the texture of a soufflé, Creamy Potato Casserole with just a hint of onion, and a rich compote of Hot Gingered Fruit. Spread toasty-brown Cheese Biscuits with lots of butter; then top off the meal with a glazed Cranberry Coffee Cake. Sunshine Breakfast Drink, made either with or without sherry, is a delightful fruit-based beverage to serve with the meal.

CRANBERRY COFFEE CAKE
½ cup butter or margarine, softened
1 cup sugar
2 eggs
2 cups all-purpose flour
1 teaspoon baking powder
1 teaspoon baking soda
½ teaspoon salt
1 (8-ounce) carton commercial sour cream
1 teaspoon almond extract
1 (16-ounce) can whole-berry cranberry
  sauce
½ cup chopped walnuts or pecans
Glaze (optional)

Cream butter and sugar until light and fluffy. Add eggs, one at a time, beating thoroughly after each addition. Combine flour, baking powder, soda, and salt; add to creamed mixture alternately with sour cream,

beating well after each addition. Add flavoring and mix well.

Spoon one-third of mixture into a greased and floured 10-inch tube pan. Spread one-third of cranberry sauce over batter. Repeat layers twice, ending with cranberry sauce. Sprinkle walnuts over top.

Bake at 350° for 1 hour or until cake tests done. Let cool 5 minutes before removing from pan. Drizzle glaze over top, if desired. Yield: one 10-inch cake.

Glaze:
¾ cup sifted powdered sugar
½ teaspoon almond extract
1 tablespoon warm water

Combine all ingredients; stir well. Yield: enough for one 10-inch cake.

SUNSHINE BREAKFAST DRINK
5 cups orange juice
1 cup half-and-half
1 cup cream sherry (optional)
1 (8-ounce) can crushed pineapple,
  undrained
2 bananas, cut into chunks
2 eggs
1 teaspoon vanilla extract
6 ice cubes

Blend all ingredients in container of an electric blender until smooth, blending half of each ingredient at a time. Serve immediately. Yield: 12 cups.

CREAMY POTATO CASSEROLE

9 medium baking potatoes
½ cup butter or margarine, melted
1½ cups commercial sour cream
4 green onions, chopped
1½ teaspoons salt
¼ teaspoon pepper
Green onion fan

Cover potatoes with salted water, and bring to a boil; reduce heat, and cook about 30 minutes or until tender. Cool slightly; peel and coarsely shred potatoes.

Combine potatoes and next 5 ingredients; stir well. Spoon potato mixture into a greased 2½ quart shallow casserole. Cover and bake at 350° for 20 minutes. Garnish with green onion fan. Yield: 10 servings.

SAUSAGE-CHEESE BAKE

1½ pounds bulk pork sausage
9 eggs, beaten
3 cups milk
1½ teaspoons dry mustard
1 teaspoon salt
3 slices bread, cut into ½-inch cubes
1½ cups (6 ounces) shredded Cheddar
  cheese
Green pepper rings
Fresh parsley sprigs
Cherry tomatoes

Cook sausage over medium heat until done, stirring to crumble. Drain well on paper towels; set aside.

Combine the sausage and all remaining ingredients except garnishes, mixing well. Pour into a well-greased 13- x 9- x 2-inch baking pan. Cover and refrigerate overnight. Bake at 350° for 1 hour. Garnish with a cluster of green pepper rings, parsley, and cherry tomatoes. Yield: 8 to 10 servings.

HOT GINGERED FRUIT

1 (20-ounce) can sliced pineapple,
  undrained
1 (29-ounce) can cling peach halves,
  drained
1 (16-ounce) can apricot halves, drained
1 (29-ounce) can pear halves, drained
10 maraschino cherries
¾ cup firmly packed light brown sugar
¼ cup butter or margarine, melted
½ teaspoon ground ginger

Drain pineapple, reserving 2 tablespoons juice. Pat all fruits dry with paper towels. Arrange pineapple, peaches, apricots, and pears in a 2-quart casserole; then top with cherries.

Combine brown sugar, butter, 2 tablespoons reserved pineapple juice, and ginger in a saucepan. Cook over low heat until sugar melts; pour over fruits. Bake at 350° for 30 minutes. Yield: 10 servings.

CHEESE BISCUITS

3 cups self-rising flour
½ cup shortening
1½ cups (6 ounces) shredded sharp
  Cheddar cheese
1 cup plus 2 tablespoons buttermilk
¼ teaspoon baking soda
¼ teaspoon red pepper

Combine flour and shortening in a medium bowl; cut in shortening with pastry blender until mixture resembles coarse meal. Stir in cheese.

Combine buttermilk, soda, and red pepper; pour into flour mixture, and stir well. Turn dough out onto a lightly floured surface, and knead lightly 3 or 4 times.

Roll dough to ¾-inch thickness; cut into rounds with a 1½-inch cutter. Place biscuits on lightly greased baking sheets; bake at 450° for 10 to 12 minutes. Yield: 3 dozen.

COME FOR DESSERT
ON TWELFTH NIGHT

MOCHA BUTTER CAKE
CHEERY FRUIT TART
GLAZED CAKE SQUARES
GOOD LUCK ALMOND CAKE
BROWNIE BAKED ALASKA
JELLYROLL CHARLOTTE
WALNUT CRESCENTS
COFFEE, TEA, OR CHAMPAGNE

Serve the most succulent fruits, the richest chocolate, the creamiest fillings . . . for the best party of the whole season! Let Twelfth Night be a grand finale to all holiday festivities—a time for you and your friends to indulge shamelessly in a last extravaganza of eating bliss!

Invite a group of favorite friends to come for a night of talk and to stay for dessert on January 6. Depending on how many guests are coming, you can prepare a tempting selection of several desserts.

Try the sherry-flavored Jellyroll Charlotte or the Cheery Fruit Tart with its topping of kiwi and peaches. Avid chocolate lovers will enjoy sampling the Mocha Butter Cake or the spectacular Brownie Baked Alaska. Walnut Crescents and Glazed Cake Squares with candied cherries are excellent desserts to be eaten with the fingers, and there's even a Good Luck Almond Cake—the friend who gets the slice with the almond inside will have good luck the whole year! Accompany these treats with plenty of coffee, hot tea, or even champagne.

MOCHA BUTTER CAKE
½ cup butter or margarine, softened
1 cup sugar
2 eggs
1½ cups all-purpose flour
1 teaspoon baking powder
½ teaspoon salt

½ cup milk
¾ teaspoon vanilla extract
Mocha Frosting (recipe follows)
Red, green, and yellow diced candied
  pineapple

Cream butter; gradually add sugar, beating until light and fluffy. Add eggs, one at a time, beating well after each addition.

Combine flour, baking powder, and salt; add to creamed mixture alternately with milk, beginning and ending with flour mixture. Beat at low speed of an electric mixer just until blended. Stir in vanilla.

Pour the batter into a greased and floured 8- x 4- x 3-inch loafpan. Bake at 350° for 40 to 45 minutes or until a wooden pick inserted in center comes out clean. Cool in pan 10 minutes; remove from pan and cool.

Slice cake in half, horizontally. Use about 3½ cups frosting between layers and on top and sides of cake, spreading smoothly.

Prepare a decorating bag with metal tip No. 4B or 18. Spoon about ⅔ cup frosting into decorating bag and pipe a shell border around bottom edge of cake. Prepare another decorating bag with metal tip No. 8B. Spoon about ¾ cup frosting into decorating bag and pipe large rosettes in rows to cover top of cake. (Spoon on dollops of frosting instead of piping rosettes, if desired.) Place a small piece of candied pineapple on top of each rosette. Chill until ready to serve. Yield: one 8-inch loaf.

Mocha Frosting:
1 cup butter or margarine, softened
6¾ cups sifted powdered sugar
⅓ cup water
2 tablespoons coffee-flavored liqueur or
  strong coffee
½ cup plus 1 tablespoon sifted cocoa

Cream butter; gradually add sugar alternately with water, beginning and ending with sugar. Add coffee-flavored liqueur and cocoa, beating well. Yield: about 5 cups.

Mocha Butter Cake is at its best when served with a cup of hot tea or coffee.

CHEERY FRUIT TART

1½ cups all-purpose flour
½ teaspoon baking powder
½ teaspoon salt
¼ cup butter or margarine
¼ cup shortening
4 to 6 tablespoons milk
Cream Filling (recipe follows)
1 (16-ounce) can sliced peaches, drained
3 kiwi fruits, peeled and sliced

Combine flour, baking powder, and salt in a bowl; cut in butter and shortening with a pastry blender until mixture resembles coarse meal. Sprinkle milk evenly over surface; stir with a fork until dry ingredients are moistened. Shape dough into a ball; chill at least 1 hour.

Roll dough to a ⅛-inch thickness on a lightly floured surface. Fit pastry to an 11- x 7½- x 1-inch tart pan, trimming edges to fit pan. Bake at 425° for 10 to 12 minutes or until lightly browned. Let cool completely on a wire rack.

Spread cream filling over pastry, and arrange fruit in alternating rows over filling. Yield: 16 servings.

Cream Filling:

3 egg yolks
¼ cup plus 1 tablespoon sugar
3 tablespoons all-purpose flour
½ teaspoon vanilla extract
1 cup milk
3½ tablespoons butter or margarine, softened

Combine egg yolks, sugar, flour, and vanilla in a medium saucepan; stir until well blended. Stir in milk; cook over medium heat, stirring constantly, just until mixture comes to a boil. Reduce heat, and simmer 1 minute. Let cool to lukewarm; add butter. Stir until butter melts; cover and refrigerate until thoroughly chilled. Yield: 1½ cups.

Cheery Fruit Tart has a creamy filling covered with rows of sliced peaches and exotic kiwi. Glazed Cake Squares have a garnish of candied cherries.

GLAZED CAKE SQUARES

½ cup shortening
1 cup sugar
2 eggs
1½ cups sifted cake flour
1¼ teaspoons baking powder
¼ teaspoon salt
½ cup milk
½ teaspoon almond extract
½ teaspoon vanilla extract
Glaze (recipe follows)
Sliced almonds, toasted
Candied red and green cherries

Cream shortening; gradually add sugar, beating until light and fluffy. Add eggs, one at a time, beating well after each addition.

Combine flour, baking powder, and salt; add to creamed mixture alternately with milk, beginning and ending with the flour mixture. Mix well after each addition. Stir in flavorings.

Pour the batter into a greased and floured 13- x 9- x 2-inch baking pan. Bake at 350° for 25 minutes or until a wooden pick inserted in center comes out clean. Cool in pan 10 minutes; invert on a wire rack to cool completely. Drizzle with glaze and decorate with almonds and cherries. Cut into squares. Yield: 24 servings.

Glaze:
1 cup sifted powdered sugar
2 teaspoons milk

Combine sugar and milk, stirring until smooth. Yield: about ⅓ cup.

GOOD LUCK ALMOND CAKE

1 (2½-ounce) package slivered almonds, chopped
⅓ cup butter or margarine, softened
⅓ cup shortening
1¼ cups sugar
3 eggs, separated
1 teaspoon grated lemon rind
2 tablespoons lemon juice
1 teaspoon vanilla extract
1 teaspoon almond extract
2⅓ cups all-purpose flour
2 teaspoons baking powder
¼ teaspoon baking soda
¾ teaspoon salt
¾ cup milk
½ teaspoon cream of tartar
¼ cup sugar
1 whole almond
Apricot Glaze

Sprinkle chopped almonds into a well-greased 9-inch Bundt pan; set aside.

Cream butter and shortening; gradually add 1¼ cups sugar, beating until light and fluffy. Add egg yolks; beat well. Add lemon rind, lemon juice, and flavorings; beat well.

Combine flour, baking powder, soda, and salt; stir well. Add dry ingredients to the creamed mixture alternately with milk, beating well after each addition; set batter aside.

Beat egg whites (at room temperature) with cream of tartar until foamy. Gradually add ¼ cup sugar, beating until stiff peaks form; fold egg white mixture into reserved batter.

Pour batter into prepared Bundt pan. Press whole almond below surface of batter. Bake at 300° for 1 hour and 20 minutes or until cake tests done. Cool cake 10 minutes in pan on wire rack. Loosen edges of cake; invert on plate. Cool completely. Drizzle with Apricot Glaze. Yield: one 9-inch cake.

Apricot Glaze:
½ cup apricot preserves
2 teaspoons rum or orange juice

Strain preserves through a sieve. Add rum; stir well. Yield: about ½ cup.

BROWNIE BAKED ALASKA

1 pint strawberry ice cream, softened
1 pint lime sherbet, softened
½ cup butter or margarine
2 (1-ounce) squares unsweetened
  chocolate
1 cup sugar
½ cup all-purpose flour
1 teaspoon baking powder
2 eggs
1 teaspoon vanilla extract
1 cup chopped walnuts or pecans
5 egg whites
1 cup sugar

Line a 1-quart mixing bowl (about 7 inches in diameter) with waxed paper, leaving an overhang around the edges. Pack ice cream and sherbet into bowl, one layer at a time, and freeze until very firm.

Combine butter and chocolate in top of double boiler; bring water to a boil. Reduce heat to low, and cook until chocolate melts.

Combine 1 cup sugar, flour, and baking powder in a mixing bowl; add chocolate mixture, mixing well. Add 2 eggs; beat well. Stir in vanilla and walnuts. Pour mixture into a greased and floured 8-inch round cakepan. Bake at 350° for 25 to 30 minutes. Let cool in pan 10 minutes; remove to wire rack, and allow to cool completely.

Place cake on an ovenproof wooden board or serving dish. Invert bowl of ice cream onto brownie layer, leaving waxed paper intact; remove bowl. Place ice cream-topped cake in freezer.

Prepare a decorating bag with metal tip No. 18; set aside.

Beat egg whites (at room temperature) until frothy; gradually beat in 1 cup sugar. Continue beating until stiff peaks form. Spoon about ¾ cup meringue into decorating bag. Remove ice cream-topped cake from freezer, and peel off waxed paper. Quickly spread remaining meringue over entire surface, making sure edges are sealed. Pipe meringue from decorating bag onto sides of Alaska following flower design in photograph. Pipe meringue around base.

Bake at 500° for 2 minutes or until the meringue peaks are browned. Serve immediately. Yield: 10 to 12 servings.

Note: After meringue is sealed, the dessert can be returned to freezer, uncovered, for up to 1 week and baked just before serving.

JELLYROLL CHARLOTTE

4 eggs
¾ teaspoon baking powder
¼ teaspoon salt
¾ cup sugar
¾ cup all-purpose flour
1 teaspoon lemon extract
Powdered sugar
½ cup raspberry preserves
Charlotte Filling (recipe follows)

Grease a 15- x 10- x 1-inch jellyroll pan, and line with waxed paper; grease and flour waxed paper. Set aside.

Combine eggs, baking powder, and salt; beat at high speed of an electric mixer until foamy. Gradually add ¾ cup sugar, beating until mixture is thick and lemon colored. Fold in flour and lemon extract. Spread batter evenly in prepared pan. Bake at 400° for 10 to 12 minutes.

Sift powdered sugar in a 15- x 10-inch rectangle on a linen towel. When cake is done, immediately loosen from sides of pan and turn out onto sugar. Peel off waxed paper. Starting at long end, roll up cake and towel together; cool on a wire rack, seam side down, 10 minutes.

Unroll cake; remove towel. Spread cake with preserves, and carefully reroll. Return to wire rack, and cool completely.

Slice jellyroll into 25 equal slices. Line a 2-quart glass bowl with 24 jellyroll slices, pressing them against each other to cover bottom and sides of bowl. Reserve the remaining slice for a garnish.

Spoon filling into jellyroll-lined bowl. Cover with plastic wrap and chill until set. Garnish with jellyroll slice and whipped cream reserved from filling. Yield: 12 servings.

Charlotte Filling:

1 envelope unflavored gelatin
¼ cup milk
2 eggs
1 cup sugar
¼ teaspoon salt
2 cups milk
3 tablespoons cream sherry
1 teaspoon vanilla extract
2 cups whipping cream, whipped and
    divided

    Soften gelatin in ¼ cup milk; set aside.
Combine eggs and sugar, beating until thick
and lemon colored; stir in salt and 2 cups
milk. Cook in top of double boiler, stirring
constantly, until thickened. Remove from
heat, and stir in gelatin mixture; cool.
    Stir sherry and vanilla into custard; fold in
3½ cups whipped cream, reserving remainder for garnish. Yield: 6 cups.

WALNUT CRESCENTS

2 cups all-purpose flour
2 cups finely chopped walnuts
¼ cup sugar
1 cup butter or margarine, melted
2 teaspoons vanilla extract
Powdered sugar (optional)

    Combine all ingredients except powdered
sugar; mix well. Pinch off small mounds of
dough and shape into crescents. (Dough will
be slightly crumbly.) Place on ungreased
cookie sheets.
    Bake at 325° for 18 to 20 minutes or until
golden. Cool on wire racks. Sprinkle with
powdered sugar, if desired. Yield: about 3
dozen cookies.

*Rainbow-colored sherbet is the surprise filling in this
elegant Brownie Baked Alaska. The equally showy
Jellyroll Charlotte can be made ahead and refrigerated.
Walnut Crescents are a buttery cookie with a texture
somewhat like shortbread.*

SPECIAL TREATS

MUFFIN TIN TARTS
MOLDED CHOCOLATES
CHOCOLATE ANGEL PIE

Wouldn't you love to receive a personalized greeting card made of deep, dark chocolate? Well, so would your friends! And can you think of a more enjoyable memory for the children than spending the afternoon helping Mommy make scumptious Christmas tarts? For a very special dessert, indeed, try the meringue- and nut-crusted Chocolate Angel Pie with its fluffy whipped cream filling. Part of the joy of the Christmas season comes from taking the time to do those little extras that you wouldn't do the rest of the year. Whether you call them crafts—or cooking—creating these special treats will add greatly to your holiday pleasure.

MUFFIN TIN TARTS
½ cup shortening
¾ cup sugar
1 egg
3 tablespoons orange juice
1½ tablespoons lemon juice
½ teaspoon vanilla extract
2½ cups all-purpose flour
¼ teaspoon salt
Assorted fillings and toppings

Cream shortening; gradually add sugar, beating until light and fluffy. Add egg, fruit juices, and vanilla, beating well. Combine dry ingredients; add to creamed mixture, mixing well (mixture will be very stiff). Cover and chill dough about 1 hour.

Roll dough out to ⅛-inch thickness on lightly floured waxed paper. Cut with a

Children love being able to assemble their own tarts—let them choose any fillings which appeal to their young tastes.

fluted 2½-inch cookie cutter. Press dough circles into lightly greased miniature muffin pans. Bake at 300° for 12 to 15 minutes or until lightly browned. Remove tart shells immediately from pans and let cool on wire racks. Spoon desired fillings, such as pudding, softened cream cheese, canned pie filling, mincemeat, and ice cream into shells. Toppings may include slices of fruit, nuts, preserves, chocolate shavings, assorted candies, or anything your child thinks is a treat! Yield: about 5½ dozen.

MOLDED CHOCOLATES
The tremendous variety of plastic molds available in many kitchen shops makes it easy to create chocolate greeting cards and other fancy candies. Once you have the molds and some basic knowledge on working with chocolates, you can use your imagination to make countless colorful treats.

The molds for this type of candymaking are usually flat. Often they are fashioned from transparent plastic which allows you to peek underneath while molding to check for unwanted air bubbles.

Semisweet or milk chocolate in chunk, block, or chip form is most often used for these projects. For a contrasting accent, mold with white chocolate; this is available at candy counters in many large department stores or gourmet shops.

If your mold needs a red bell or a green leaf, melt white chocolate and stir in paste food coloring. Don't use liquid coloring; this will cause the chocolate to thicken and form lumps.

Chocolate-flavored compounds, often called summer coatings, are also available in some areas. Because they harden quickly after molding, are not hard to melt, and are more resistant to heat and humidity than real chocolate, these compounds make candymaking even easier.

Summer coatings are available in a rainbow of colors in either the chunk or wafer form. The advantage of the wafer form is that you don't have to chop it before melting. If you use large chunks of chocolate, chop or grate them before beginning your molding project.

Molding Chocolate

Because chocolate scorches easily, heat it in a double boiler over hot, but not boiling, water until almost melted. Remove the top of the double boiler from water, and stir until chocolate melts completely.

When melting small amounts of many different colors, use jars—one for each color—set into water in an electric skillet (to simulate a double boiler). Let the jars remain in warm water while you paint designs. If candy hardens too much, reheat slowly just until melted.

Summer coatings are available in a pastel rainbow of colors—ready to be melted and formed in any mold you choose.

Paint details directly onto mold using desired color of melted candy; fill remainder of mold with chocolate.

Be careful not to let any steam or water droplets get into the chocolate or summer coating, or it will thicken too much. All cooking utensils should be absolutely dry.

If you're using only one color per mold, simply spoon in the melted chocolate. Greasing the mold is not necessary and would harm the finished appearance of the candy. Underfill rather than overfill the mold so the finished candy won't have a base larger than the design. Tap the mold on the table to level it and to bring bubbles to the surface. Let chocolate harden (refrigerate or

A handmade chocolate card makes a thoughtful and delicious Christmas greeting.

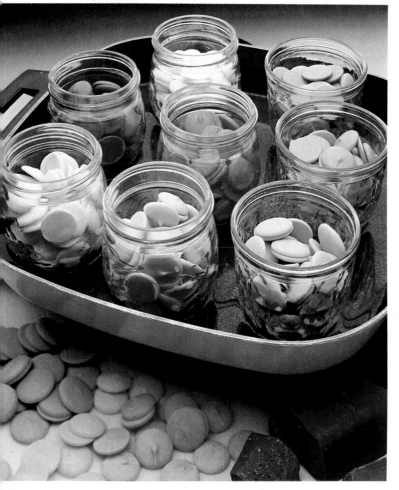

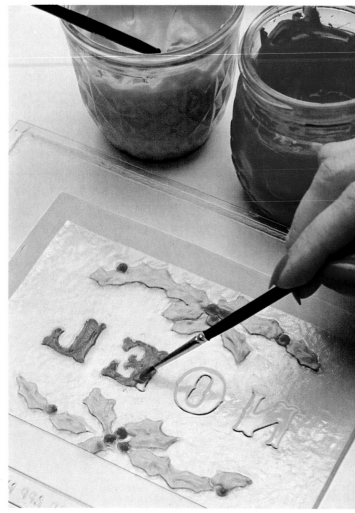

120

freeze to hasten the process); then invert the mold and tap it gently to release the candy.

For a multicolored mold, use a small paintbrush to paint details directly onto the mold. Freeze mold a few minutes after painting each color to harden candy so that the first color won't run when you paint the next. Use good quality brushes that won't lose their bristles in use, with a separate brush for each color.

After the colors are painted into the mold, spoon in enough melted chocolate to fill the mold; then freeze. Release the candy and store in a cool dry place, away from extremes in temperature. If chocolate becomes soft at room temperature, refrigerate it until ready to serve.

Molds made with real chocolate can develop "bloom", a gray discoloration on the surface of the chocolate, if exposed to extremes in temperature. This affects only the appearance, not the flavor.

CHOCOLATE ANGEL PIE

2 egg whites
⅛ teaspoon salt
⅛ teaspoon cream of tartar
½ cup sugar
½ teaspoon vanilla extract
½ cup finely chopped walnuts or pecans
1 (4-ounce) package sweet baking chocolate
3 tablespoons water
1 teaspoon vanilla extract
1 cup whipping cream, whipped

Beat egg whites (at room temperature), salt, and cream of tartar until foamy. Gradually add sugar, 2 tablespoons at a time, beating until stiff peaks form. Fold in ½ teaspoon vanilla and walnuts or pecans. Spoon the meringue into a lightly greased 8-inch pieplate. Use a spoon to shape meringue into a pie shell, swirling sides ½-inch above edge of pieplate. Bake at 300° for 50 to 55 minutes. Cool.

Molds are also available in holiday designs for smaller, bite-size candies.

Combine chocolate and water in a small saucepan; cook over low heat, stirring constantly, until melted and smooth. Stir in 1 teaspoon vanilla; cool. Fold in whipped cream; spoon into meringue shell. Refrigerate at least 2 hours. Yield: one 8-inch pie.

PATTERNS

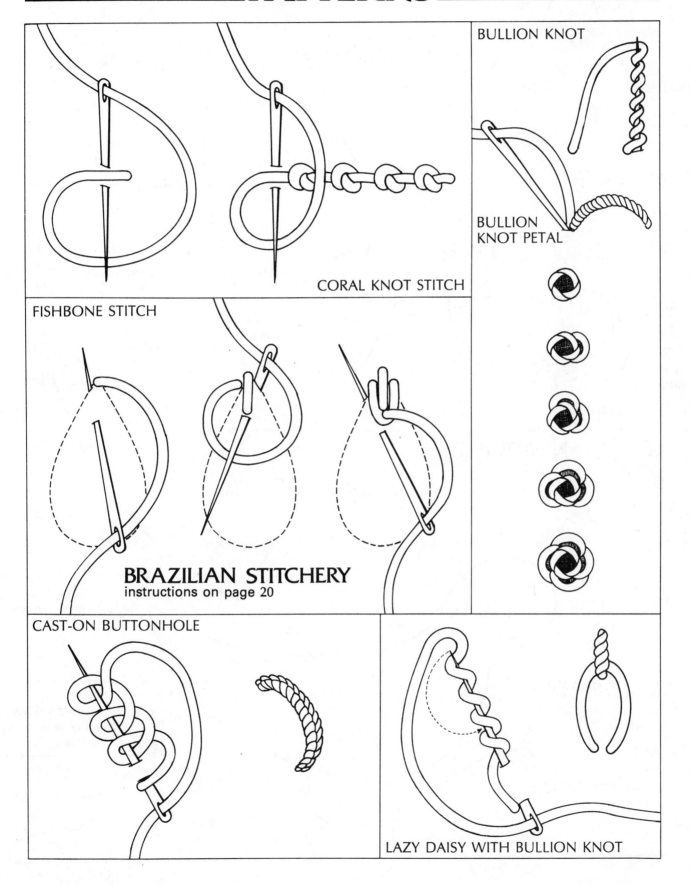

BULLION KNOT

BULLION KNOT PETAL

CORAL KNOT STITCH

FISHBONE STITCH

BRAZILIAN STITCHERY
instructions on page 20

CAST-ON BUTTONHOLE

LAZY DAISY WITH BULLION KNOT

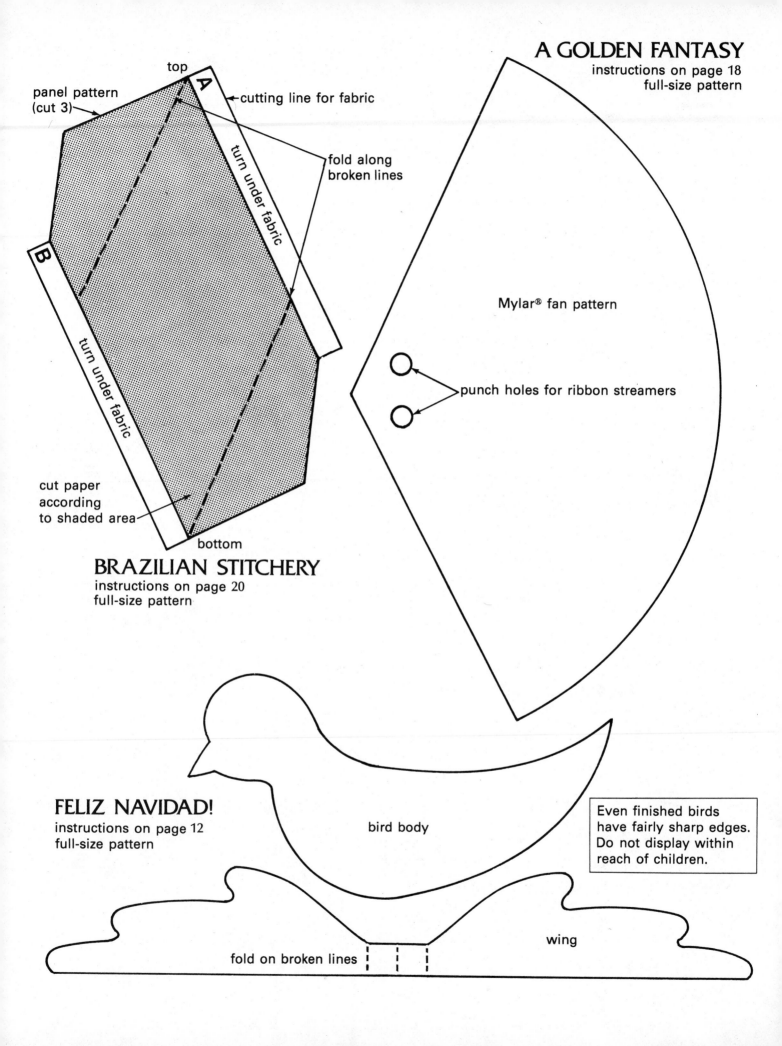

panel pattern
(cut 3)

top

A

cutting line for fabric

turn under fabric

fold along
broken lines

B

turn under fabric

cut paper
according
to shaded area

bottom

BRAZILIAN STITCHERY
instructions on page 20
full-size pattern

A GOLDEN FANTASY
instructions on page 18
full-size pattern

Mylar® fan pattern

punch holes for ribbon streamers

FELIZ NAVIDAD!
instructions on page 12
full-size pattern

bird body

wing

Even finished birds
have fairly sharp edges.
Do not display within
reach of children.

fold on broken lines

CHRISTMAS CARDINALS

instructions on page 31
full-size pattern

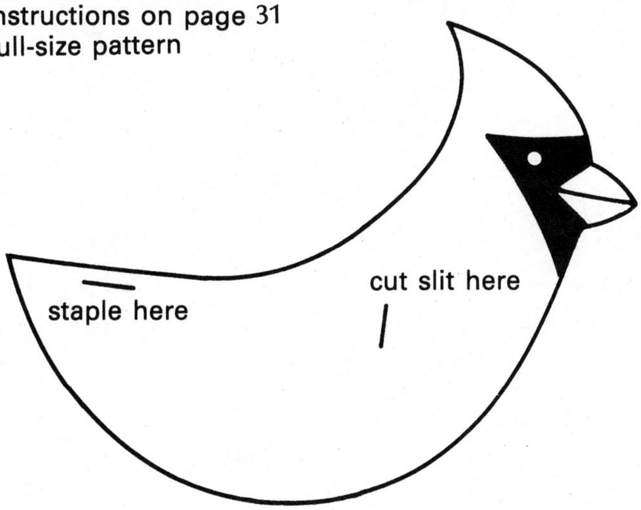

staple here

cut slit here

STARLIGHT STARBRIGHT

PILLOW COVER APPLIQUÉS
instructions on page 17
full-size pattern

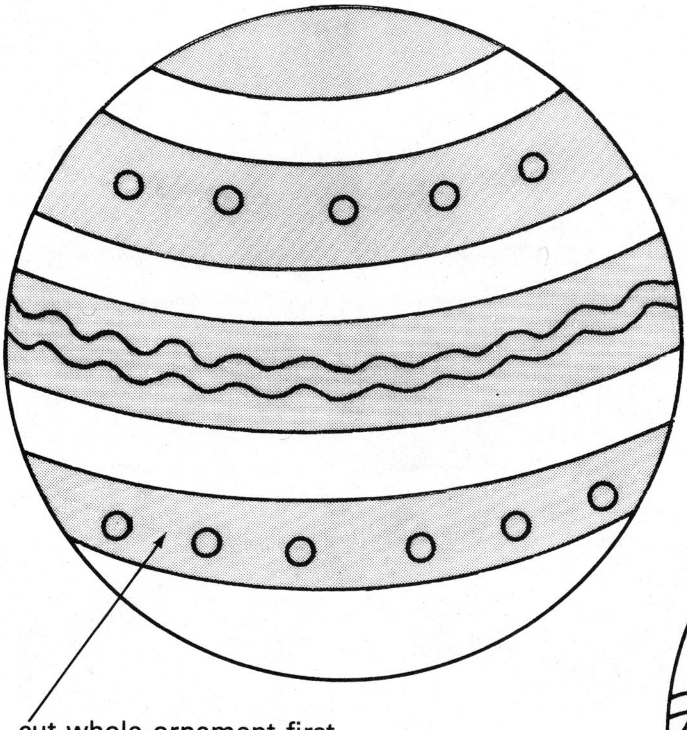

cut whole ornament first
appliqué shaded areas in contrasting colors
position trim as shown

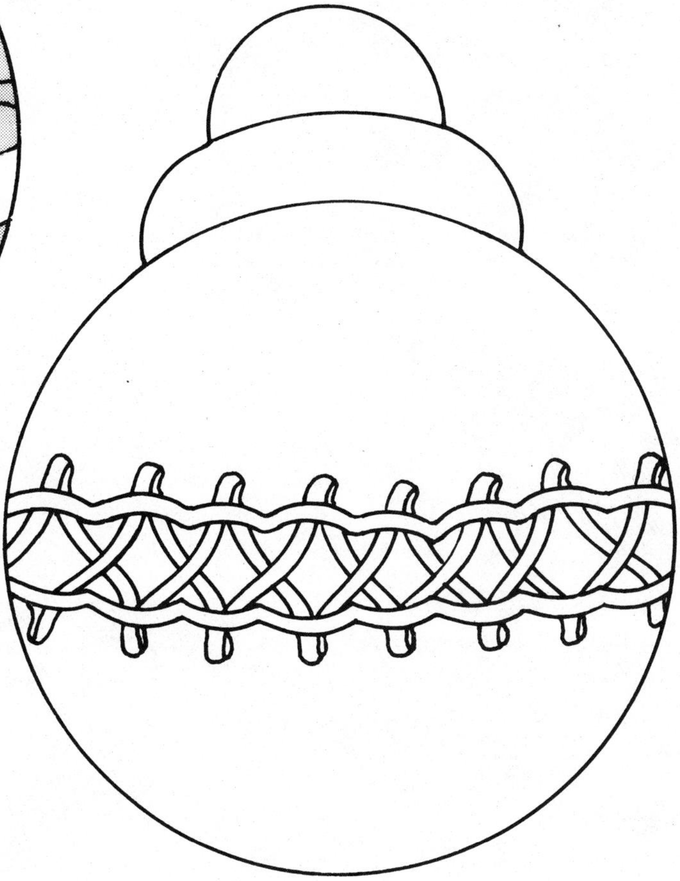

CROSS-STITCH AN HEIRLOOM
instructions on page 2

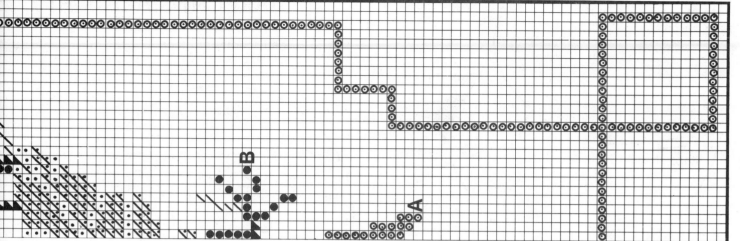

Match A and B for correct placement of border

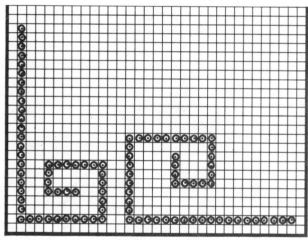

Left Corner Motif

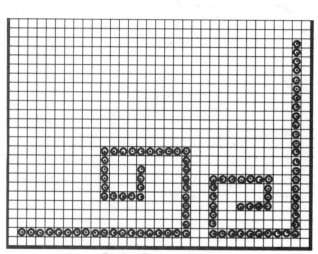

Right Corner Motif

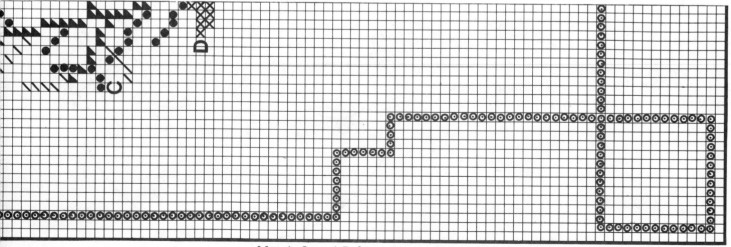

Match C and D for correct placement of border

center line

center line

dark red
bright red
peach
yellow
yellow-green
pale green
emerald green
dark green
avocado
brown

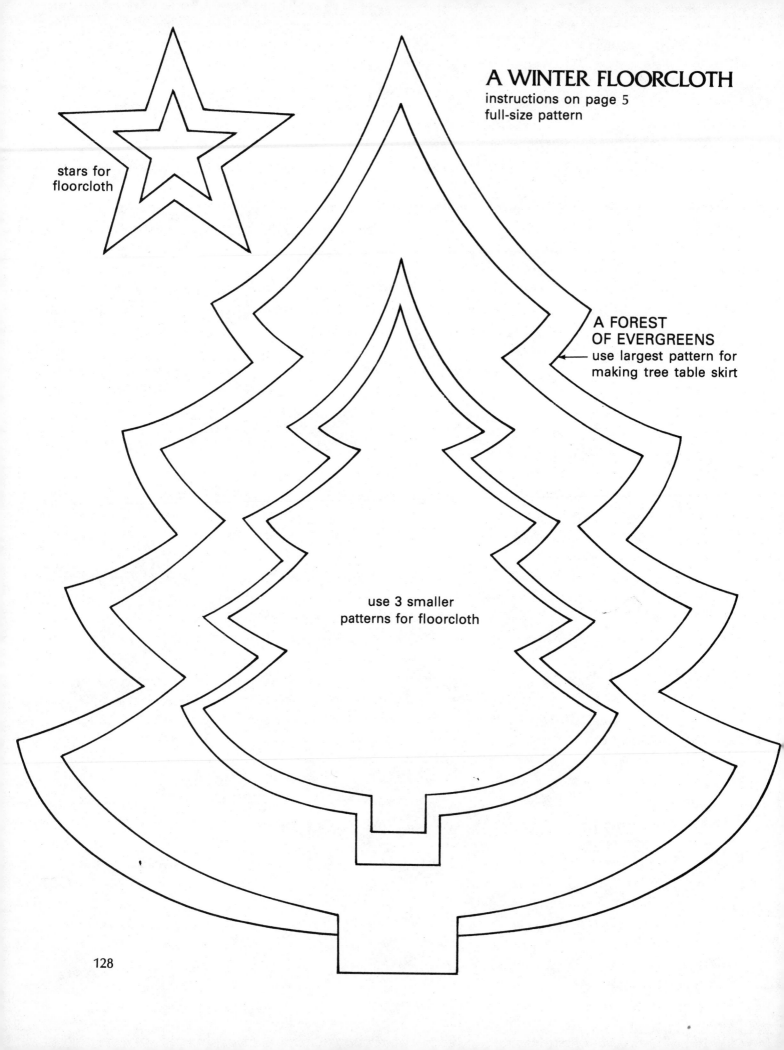

stars for
floorcloth

A WINTER FLOORCLOTH
instructions on page 5
full-size pattern

A FOREST
OF EVERGREENS
← use largest pattern for
making tree table skirt

use 3 smaller
patterns for floorcloth

128

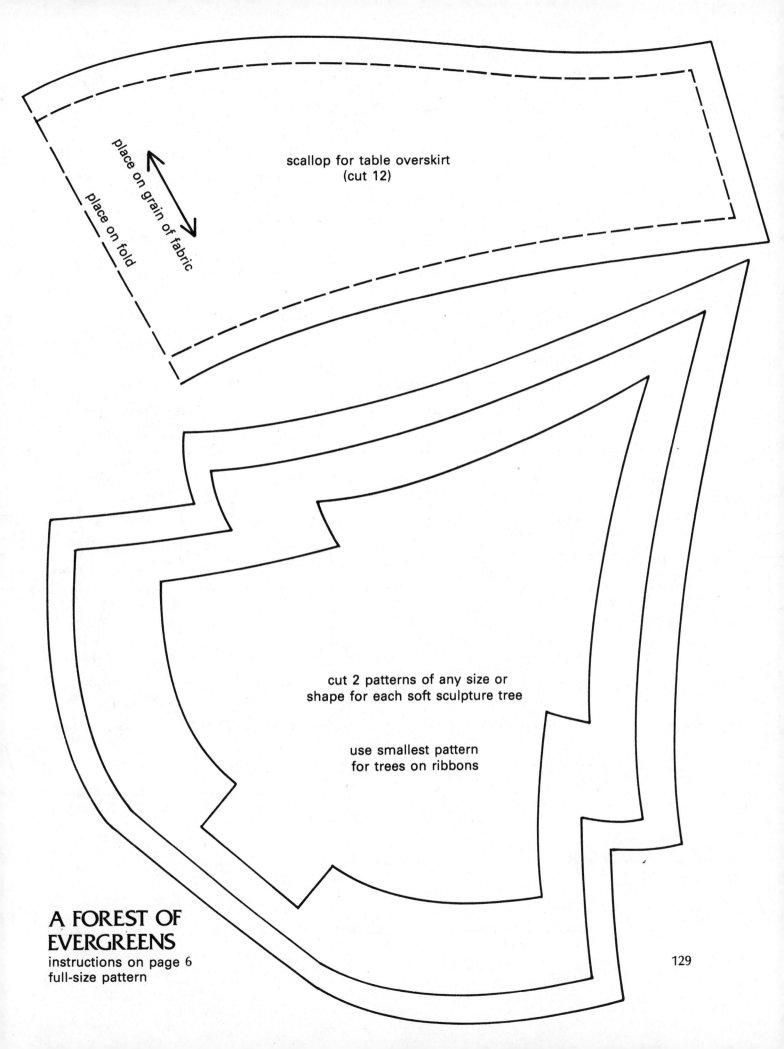

scallop for table overskirt
(cut 12)

place on grain of fabric

place on fold

cut 2 patterns of any size or
shape for each soft sculpture tree

use smallest pattern
for trees on ribbons

A FOREST OF
EVERGREENS
instructions on page 6
full-size pattern

129

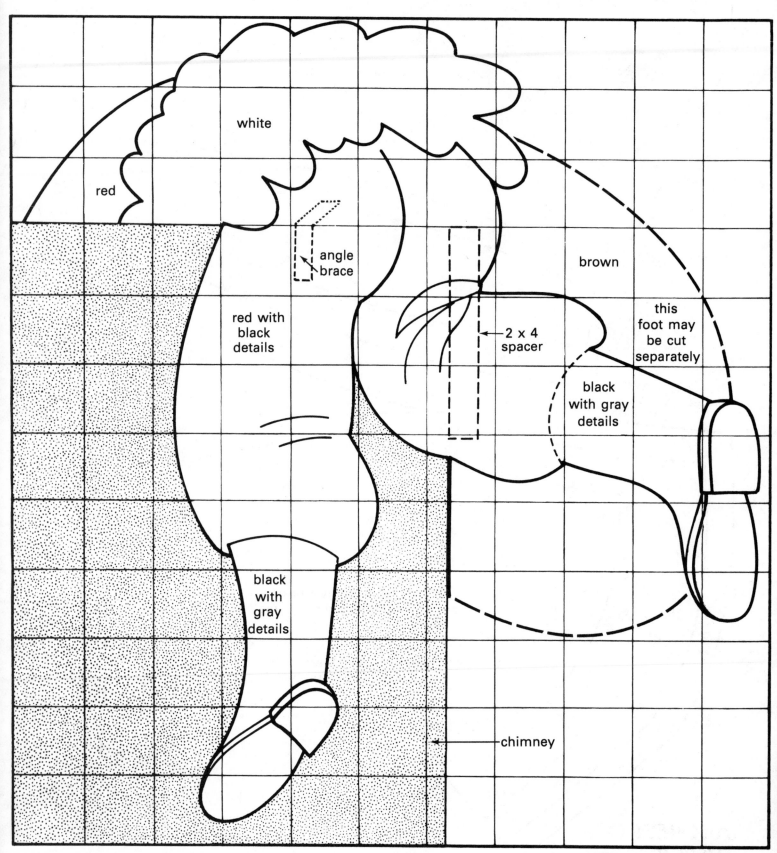

white

red

angle
brace

red with
black
details

brown

2 x 4
spacer

this
foot may
be cut
separately

black
with gray
details

black
with
gray
details

chimney

scale: 1 square equals 4"

DOWN
THROUGH
THE CHIMNEY

instructions on page 38
scale: 1 square equals 4″

increase pattern to full-size

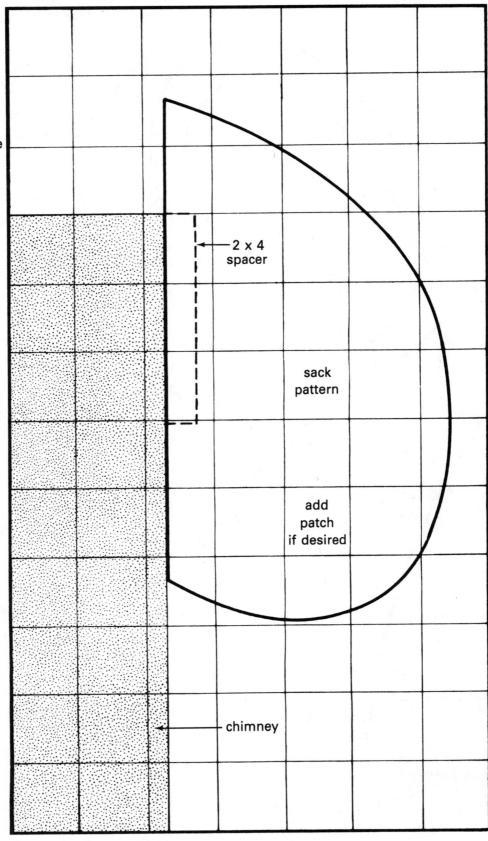

2 x 4
spacer

sack
pattern

add
patch
if desired

chimney

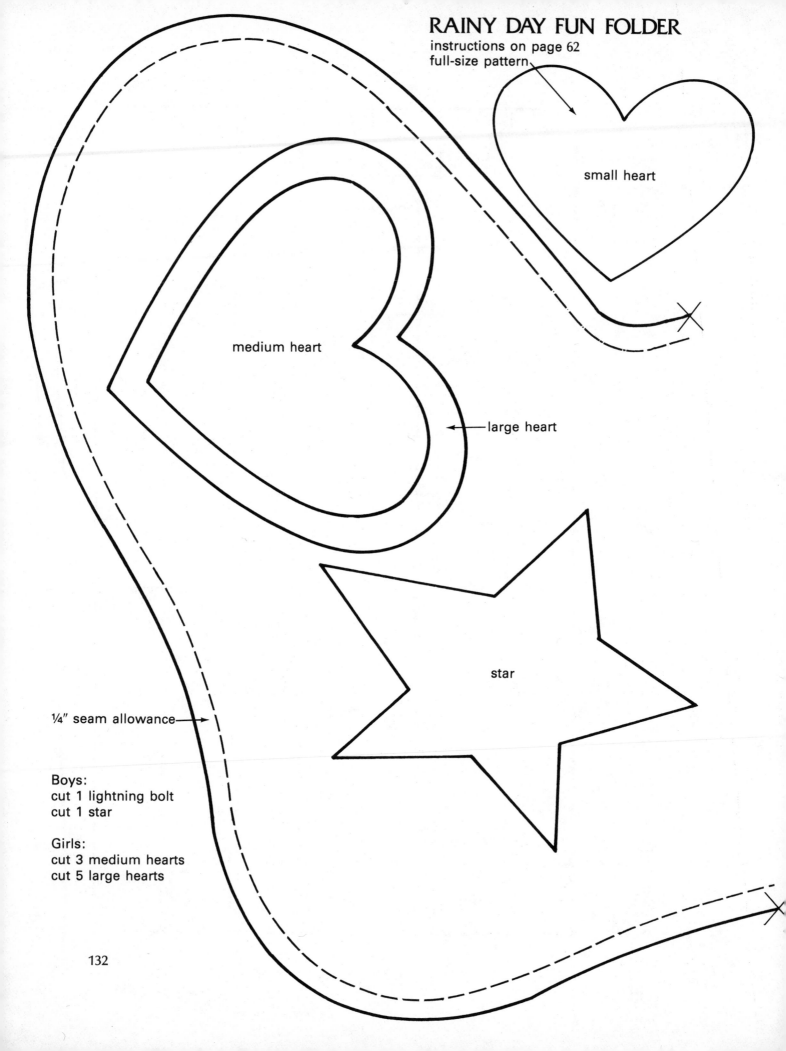

RAINY DAY FUN FOLDER
instructions on page 62
full-size pattern

small heart

medium heart

large heart

star

¼" seam allowance

Boys:
cut 1 lightning bolt
cut 1 star

Girls:
cut 3 medium hearts
cut 5 large hearts

132

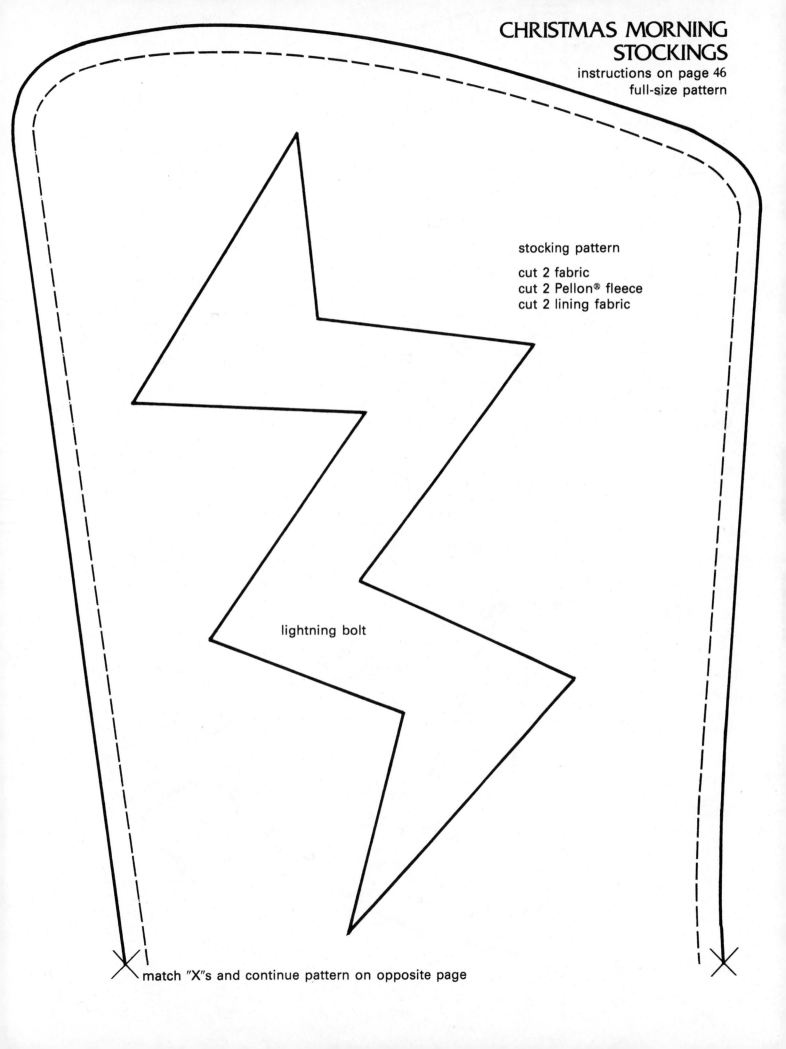

CHRISTMAS MORNING
STOCKINGS
instructions on page 46
full-size pattern

stocking pattern

cut 2 fabric
cut 2 Pellon® fleece
cut 2 lining fabric

lightning bolt

match "X"s and continue pattern on opposite page

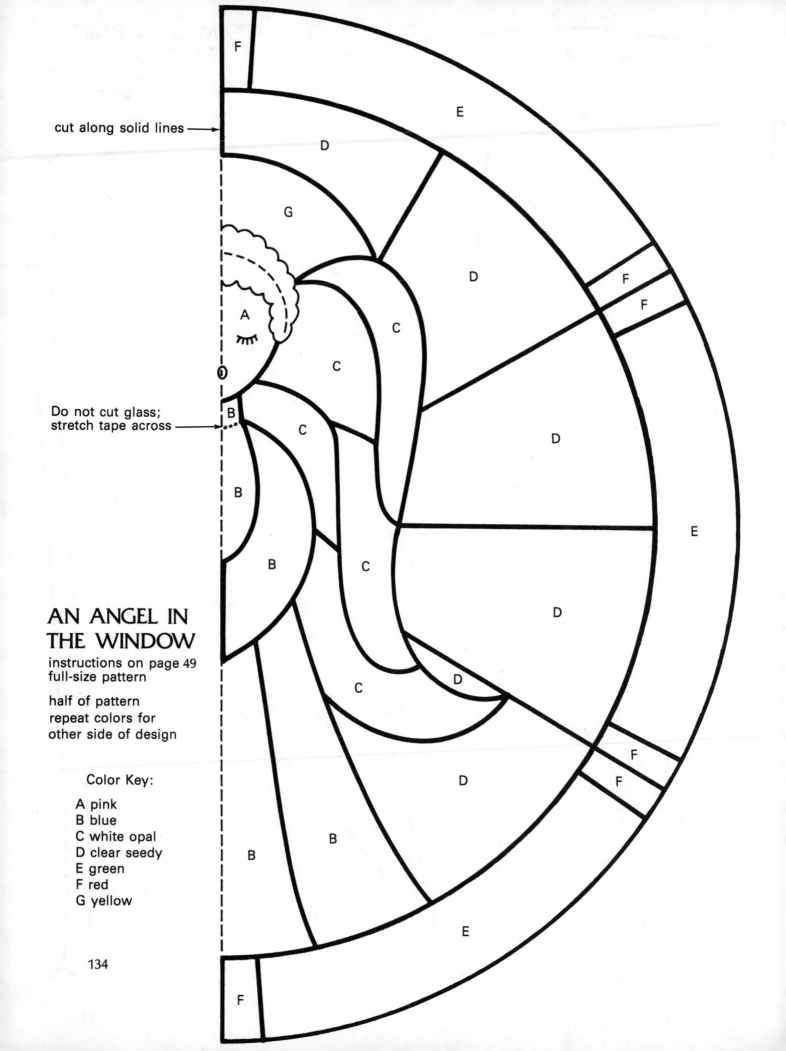

cut along solid lines →

Do not cut glass;
stretch tape across →

AN ANGEL IN THE WINDOW

instructions on page 49
full-size pattern

half of pattern
repeat colors for
other side of design

Color Key:

A pink
B blue
C white opal
D clear seedy
E green
F red
G yellow

134

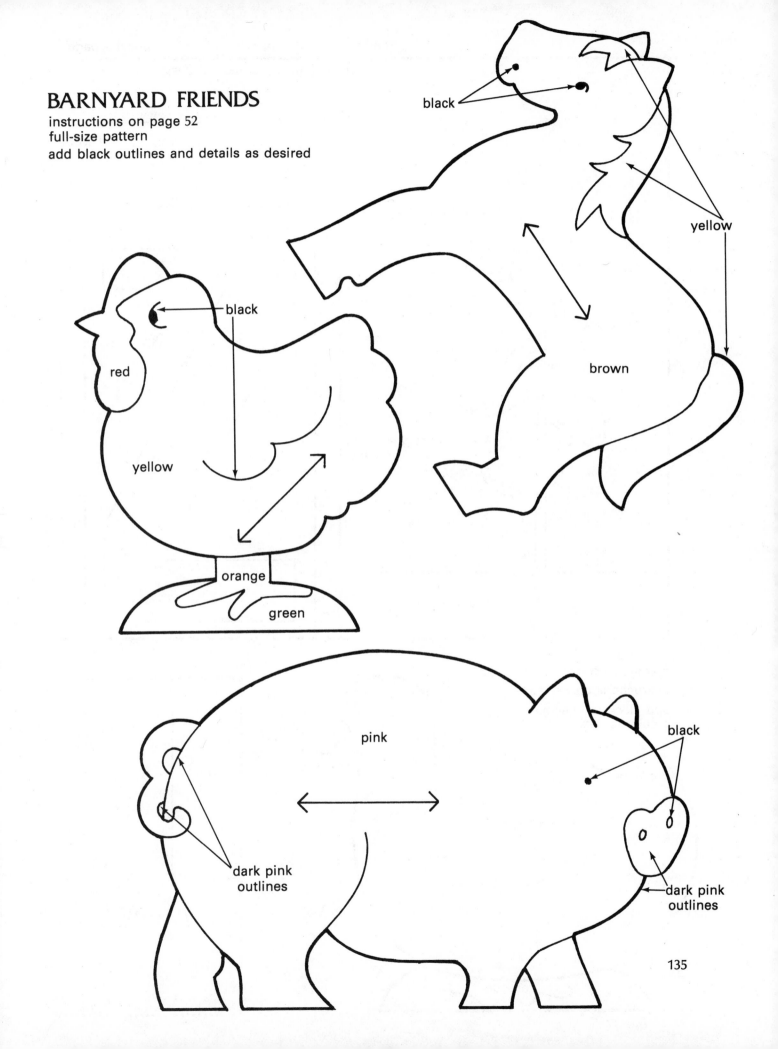

BARNYARD FRIENDS
instructions on page 52
full-size pattern
add black outlines and details as desired

black

yellow

black

red

brown

yellow

orange

green

pink

black

dark pink
outlines

dark pink
outlines

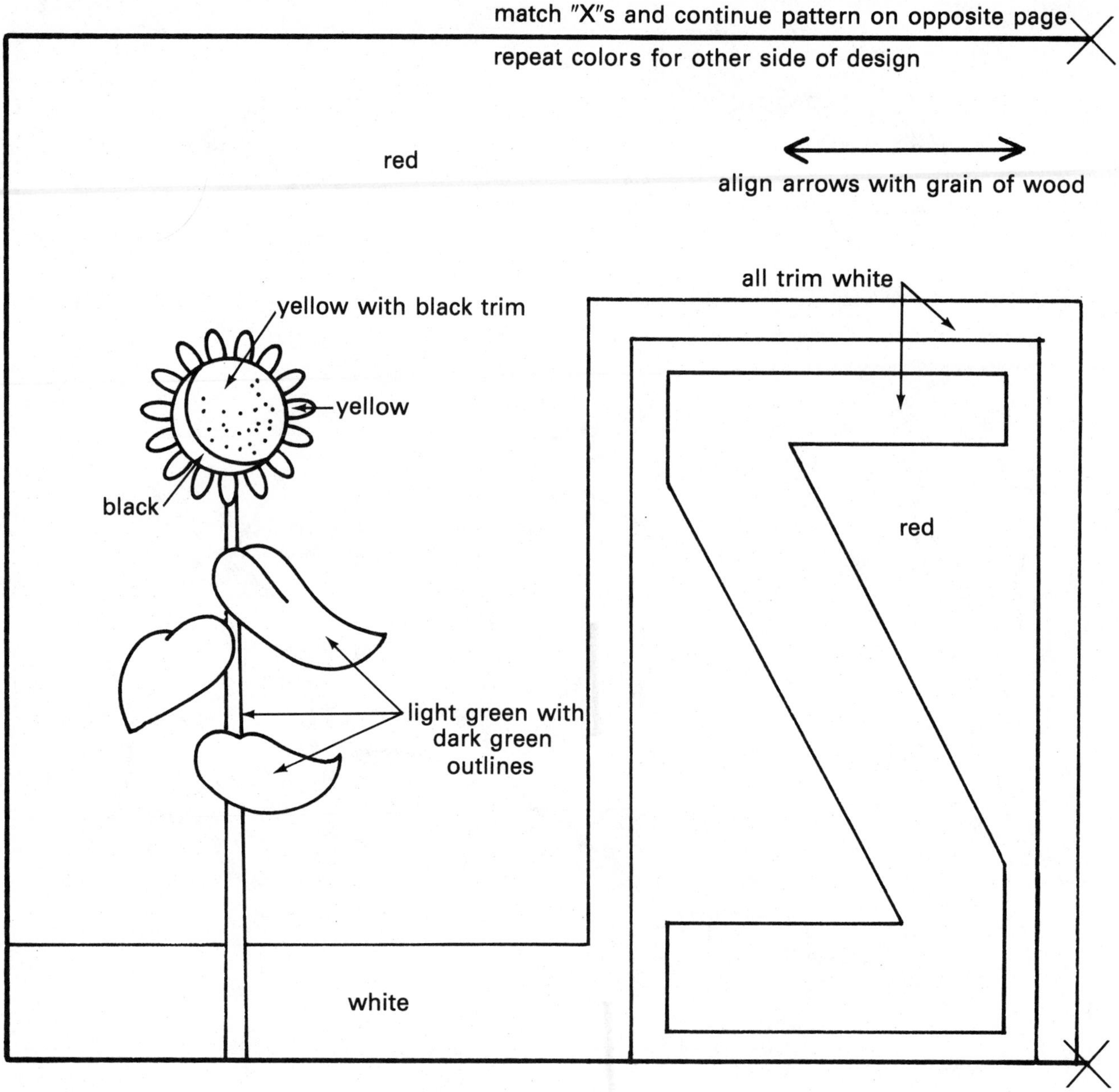
match "X"s and continue pattern on opposite page
repeat colors for other side of design
red
align arrows with grain of wood
all trim white
yellow with black trim
yellow
black
red
light green with dark green outlines
white

BARNYARD FRIENDS
instructions on page 52
add black outlines and details as desired

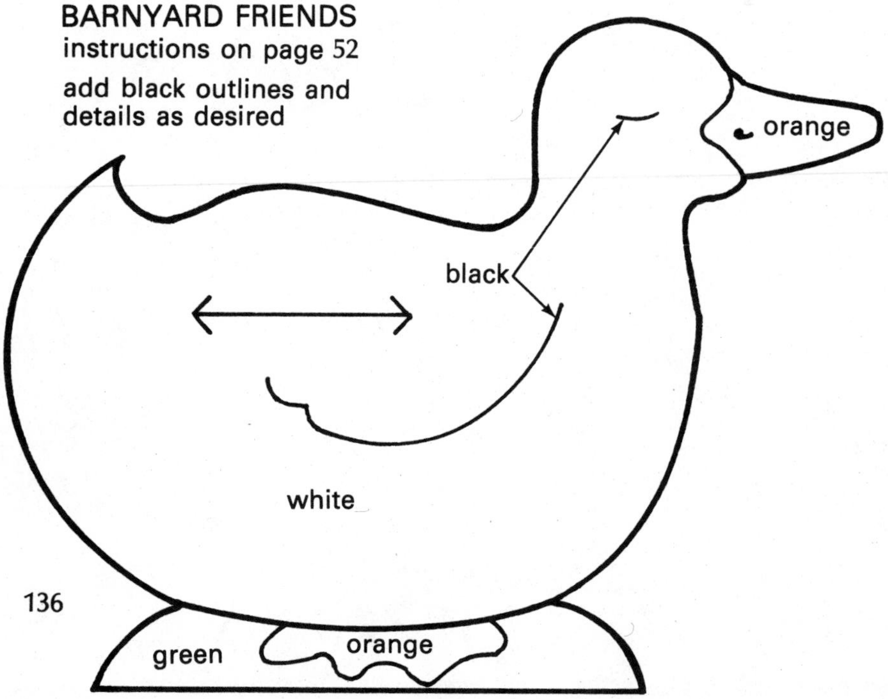
orange
black
white
green
orange

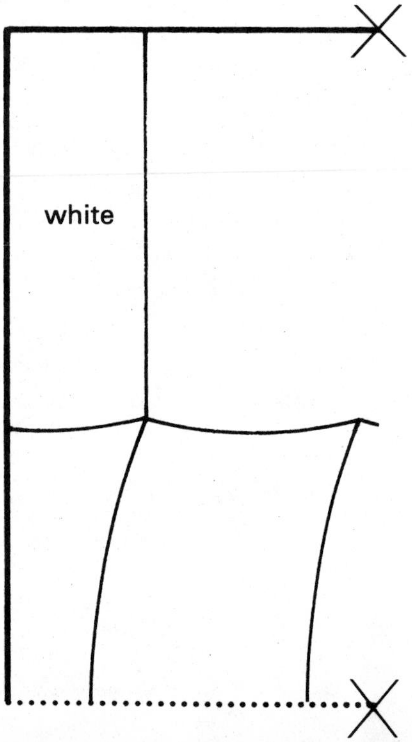
white

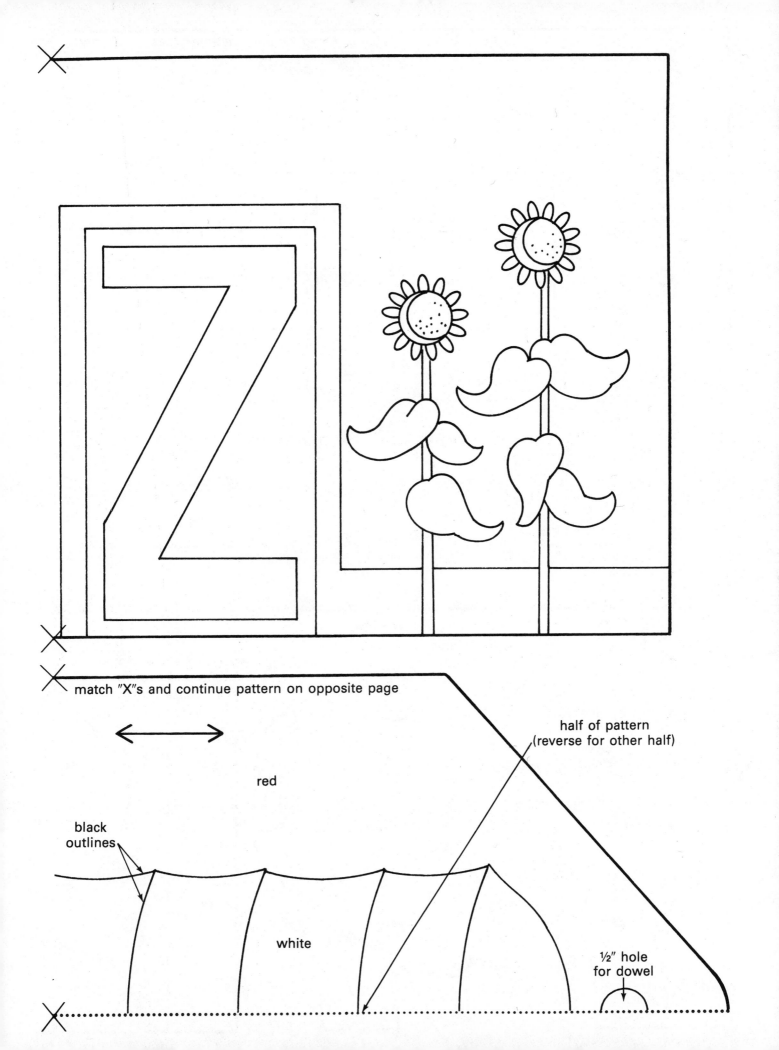

match "X"s and continue pattern on opposite page

half of pattern
(reverse for other half)

red

black
outlines

white

½" hole
for dowel

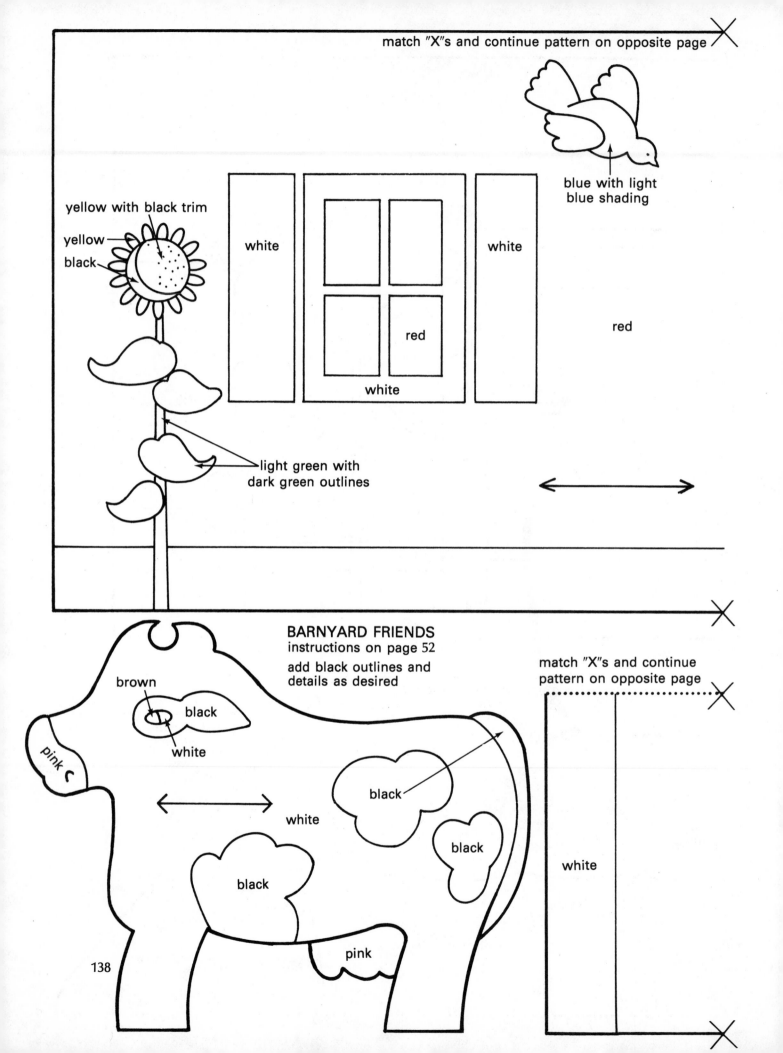

match "X"s and continue pattern on opposite page

blue with light
blue shading

yellow with black trim

yellow

black

white

white

red

red

white

light green with
dark green outlines

BARNYARD FRIENDS
instructions on page 52

add black outlines and
details as desired

match "X"s and continue
pattern on opposite page

brown

black

white

pink

black

white

black

black

white

black

pink

138

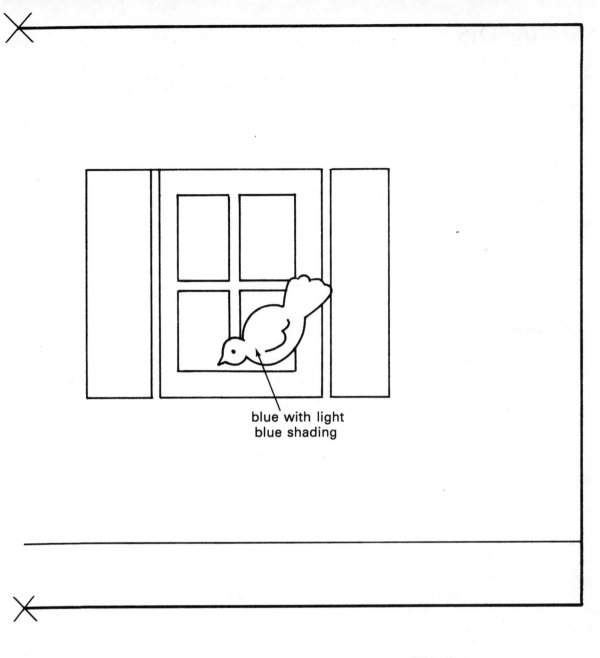

blue with light
blue shading

half of pattern (reverse for other half)

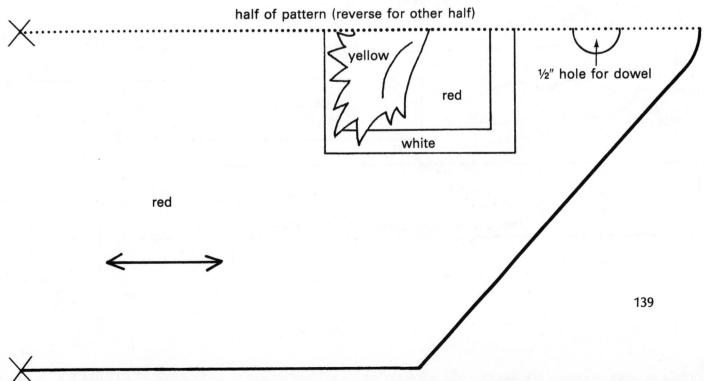

yellow

red

white

½" hole for dowel

red

139

POP-UP SANTA TOYS

instructions on page 54
full-size pattern

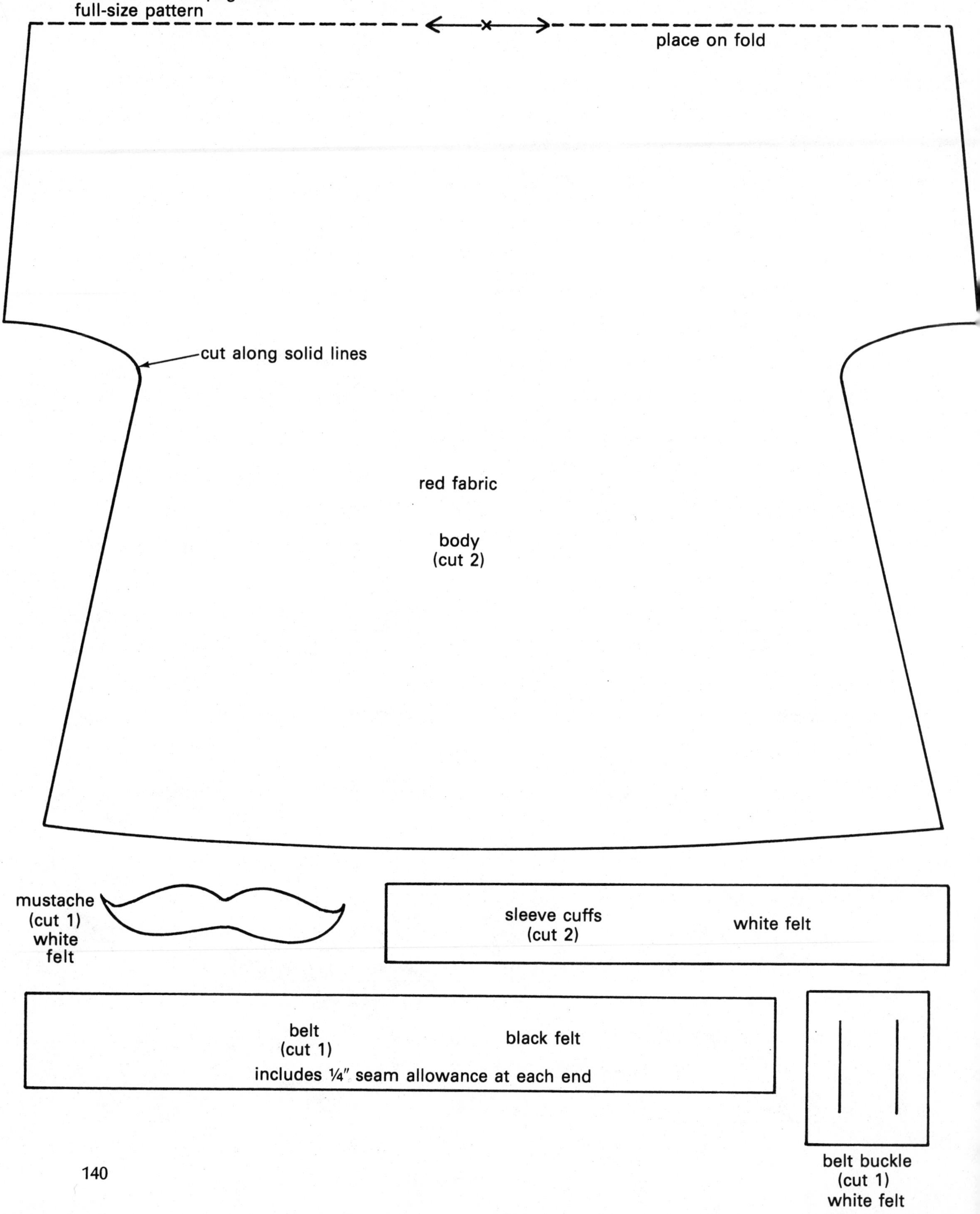

place on fold

cut along solid lines

red fabric

body
(cut 2)

mustache
(cut 1)
white
felt

sleeve cuffs
(cut 2)   white felt

belt
(cut 1)   black felt

includes ¼" seam allowance at each end

belt buckle
(cut 1)
white felt

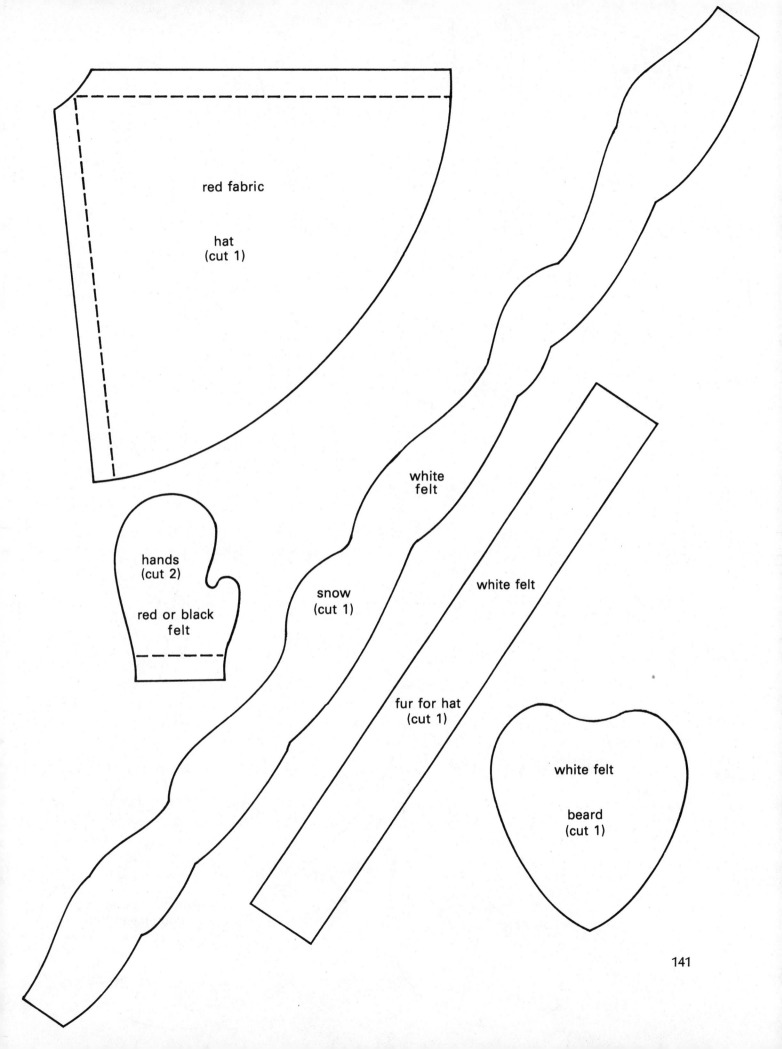

red fabric

hat
(cut 1)

hands
(cut 2)

red or black
felt

white
felt

snow
(cut 1)

white felt

fur for hat
(cut 1)

white felt

beard
(cut 1)

141

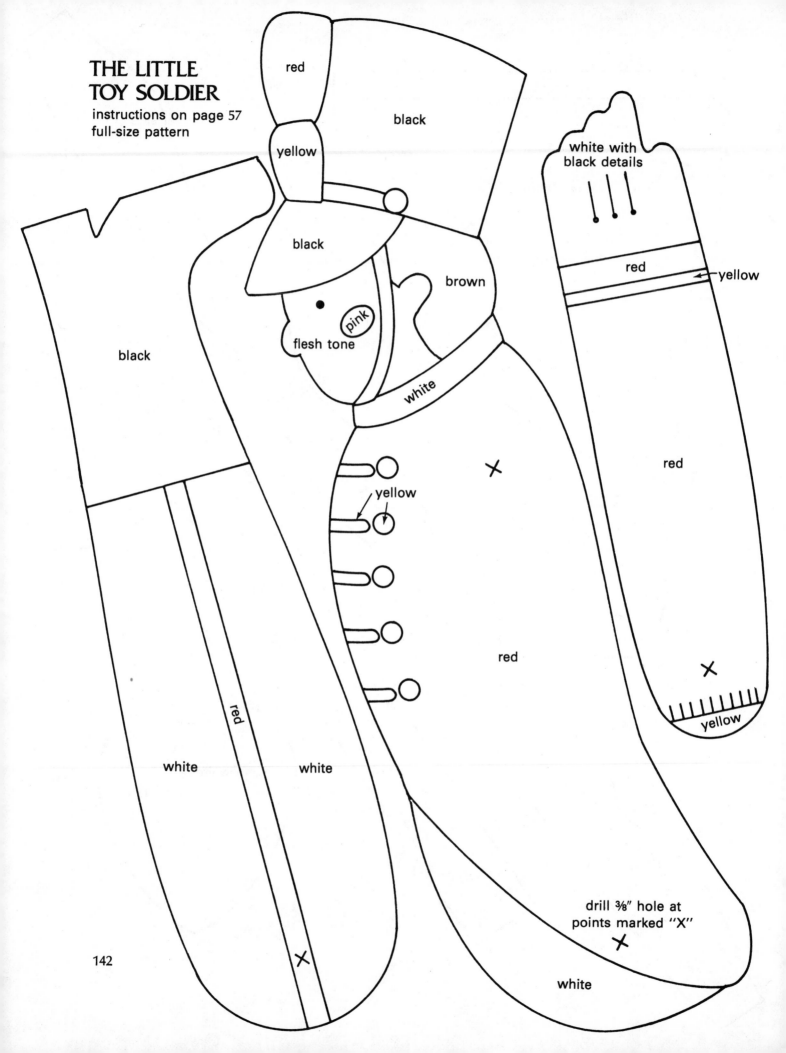

THE LITTLE TOY SOLDIER

instructions on page 57
full-size pattern

red

black

yellow

black

brown

flesh tone

pink

white

black

white

yellow

red

white

white

red

142

white with
black details

red

yellow

red

yellow

drill ⅜" hole at
points marked "X"

white

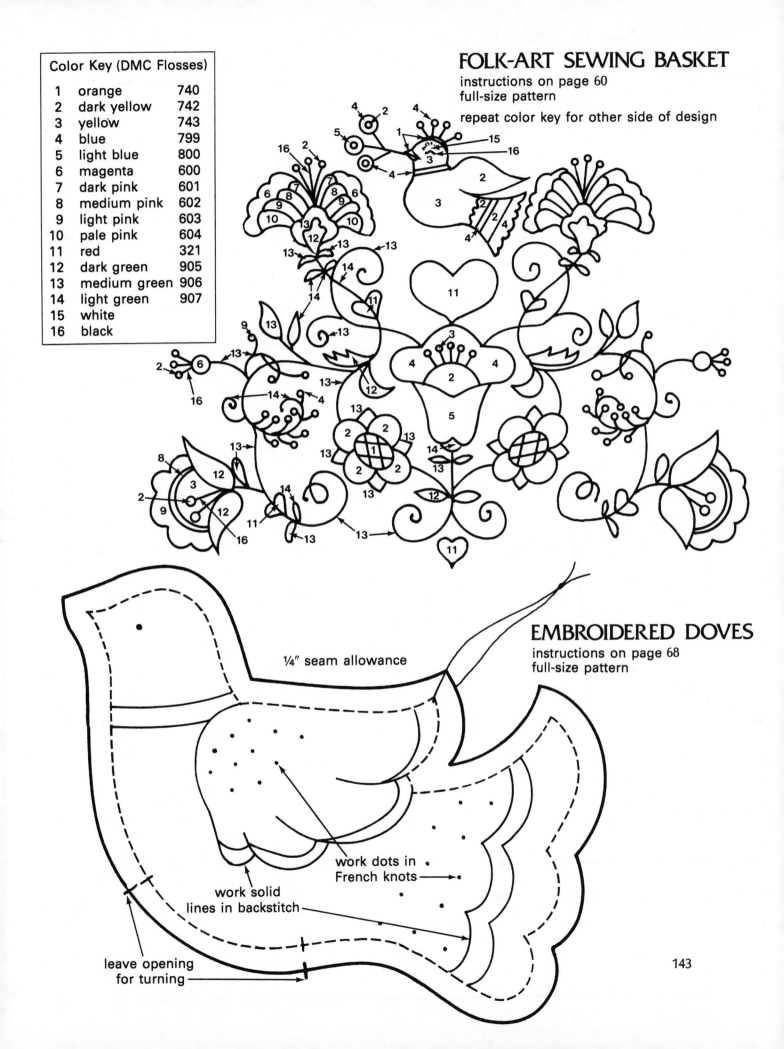

Color Key (DMC Flosses)

1	orange	740
2	dark yellow	742
3	yellow	743
4	blue	799
5	light blue	800
6	magenta	600
7	dark pink	601
8	medium pink	602
9	light pink	603
10	pale pink	604
11	red	321
12	dark green	905
13	medium green	906
14	light green	907
15	white	
16	black	

FOLK-ART SEWING BASKET
instructions on page 60
full-size pattern

repeat color key for other side of design

EMBROIDERED DOVES
instructions on page 68
full-size pattern

¼" seam allowance

work dots in
French knots

work solid
lines in backstitch

leave opening
for turning

143

STAINED GLASS IN THE KITCHEN
instructions on page 59
full-size pattern

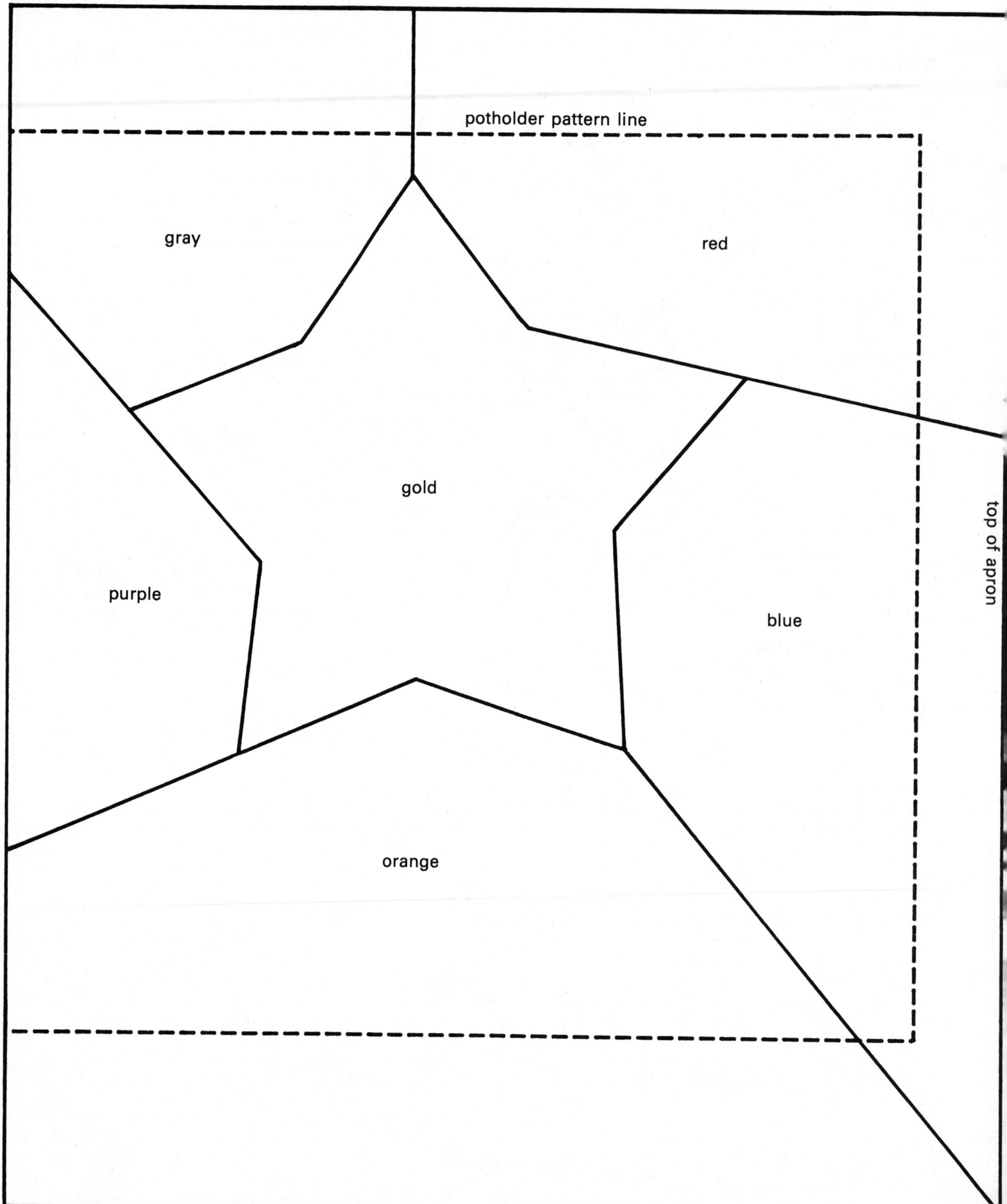

potholder pattern line

gray

red

gold

purple

blue

orange

top of apron

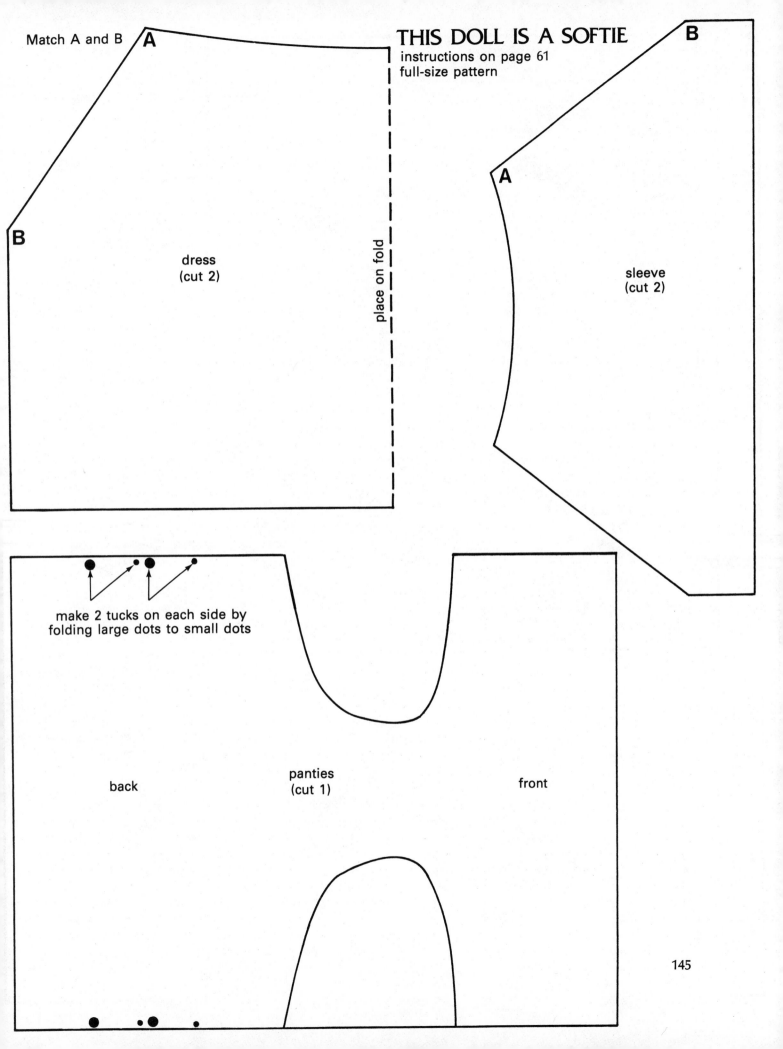

Match A and B

THIS DOLL IS A SOFTIE
instructions on page 61
full-size pattern

A

B

dress
(cut 2)

place on fold

B

A

sleeve
(cut 2)

make 2 tucks on each side by
folding large dots to small dots

back

panties
(cut 1)

front

145

Color Key
(DMC Flosses)
⊠ 415 gray
⬤ 666 red
◨ 321 dark red
◉ 353 med. pink
◪ 754 flesh
■ 310 black
⊡ white

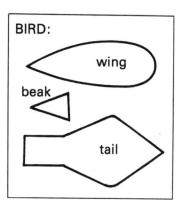

BIRD:
wing
beak
tail

SANTA HAT:
hat
hat band

LION:
face
cheeks
ears
mouth

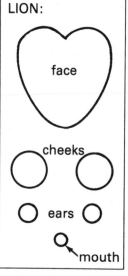

MOUSE:
cheeks
teeth
tail
ears
(cut 2)
cut

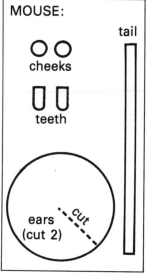

PENGUIN:
wing
feet
beak
front

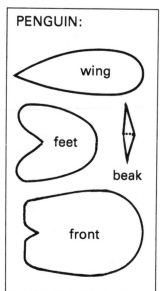

NUTTY CHRISTMAS CRITTERS
instructions on page 66   full-size patterns

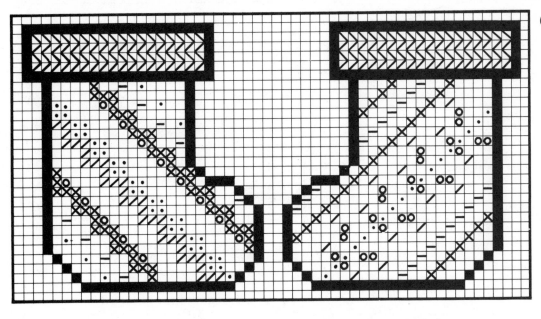

GLITTERING NEEDLEPOINT

instructions on page 69

Color Key:
- ■ gold metallic
- ◩ silver metallic
- ⊟ gold wool
- ⊡ dark green
- ⊙ light green
- ⊘ red
- ⊞ black
- ⊠ ecru

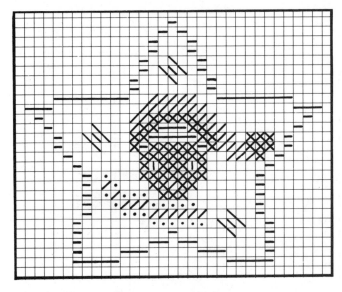

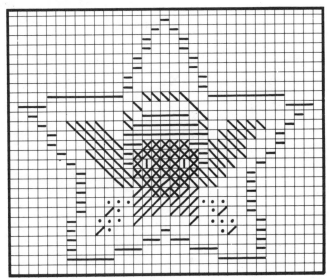

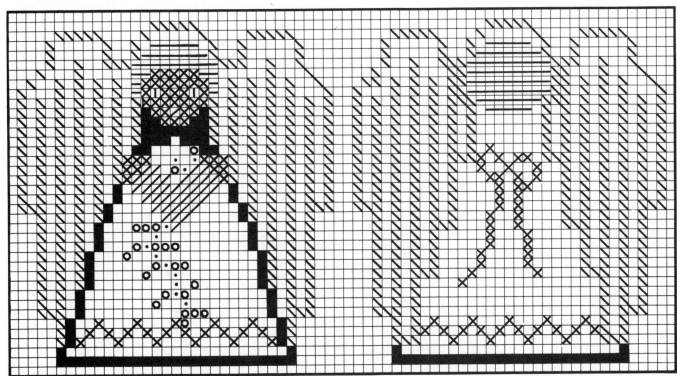

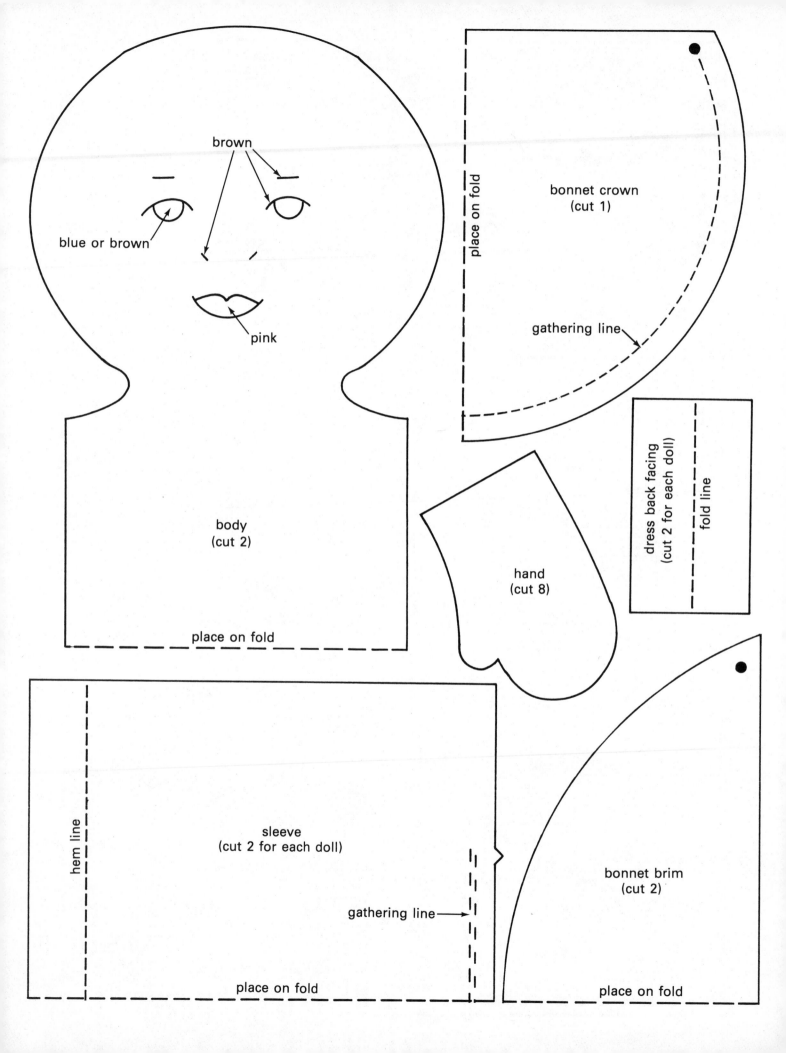

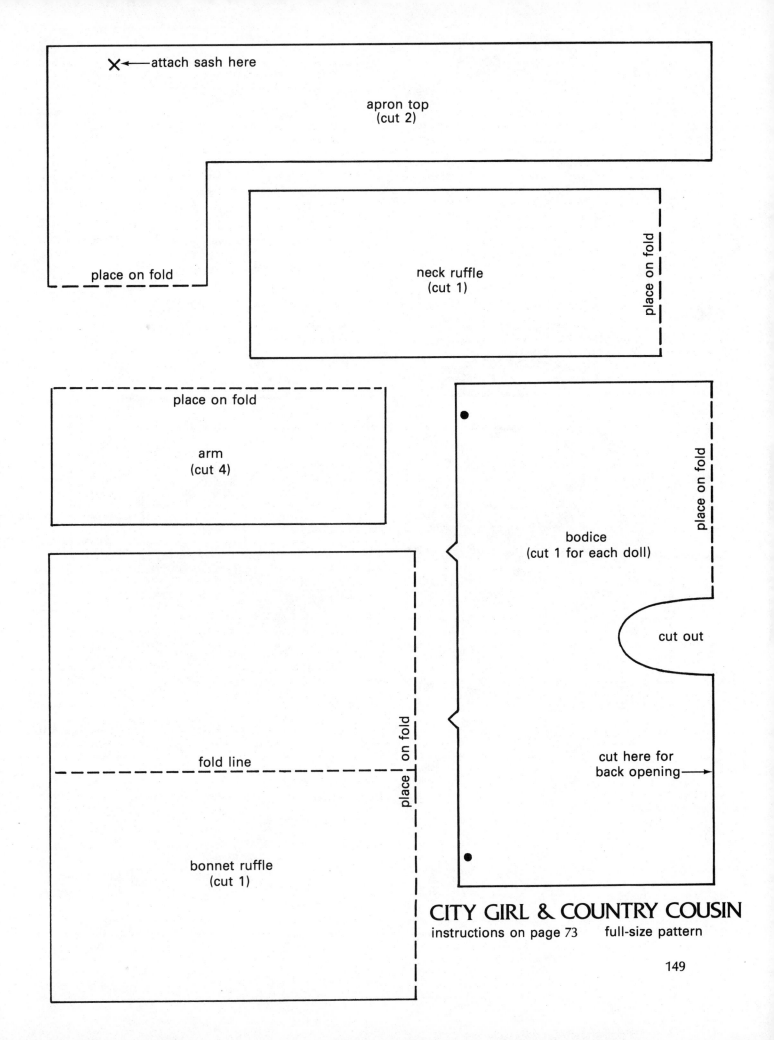

attach sash here

apron top
(cut 2)

place on fold

neck ruffle
(cut 1)

place on fold

place on fold

arm
(cut 4)

bodice
(cut 1 for each doll)

place on fold

cut out

fold line

place on fold

cut here for
back opening

bonnet ruffle
(cut 1)

CITY GIRL & COUNTRY COUSIN
instructions on page 73   full-size pattern

149

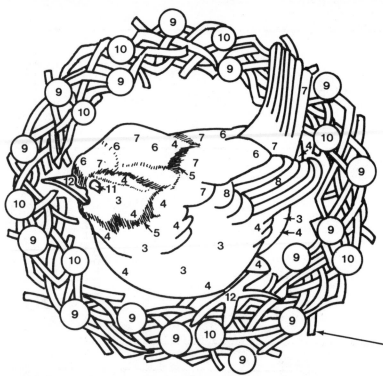

BIRD & BERRIES
instructions on page 50
full-size pattern

1 light gray-brown Persian
2 grayish-tan Persian
3 white persian
4 off-white Persian
5 dark brown Persian
6 dark spice brown Persian
7 medium spice brown Persian
8 light spice brown Persian
9 red floss, DMC #321
10 dark red floss, DMC #498
11 black floss
12 gold floss, DMC #783

dark brown floss, DMC #838
white floss

#1 and #2 used randomly in wreath

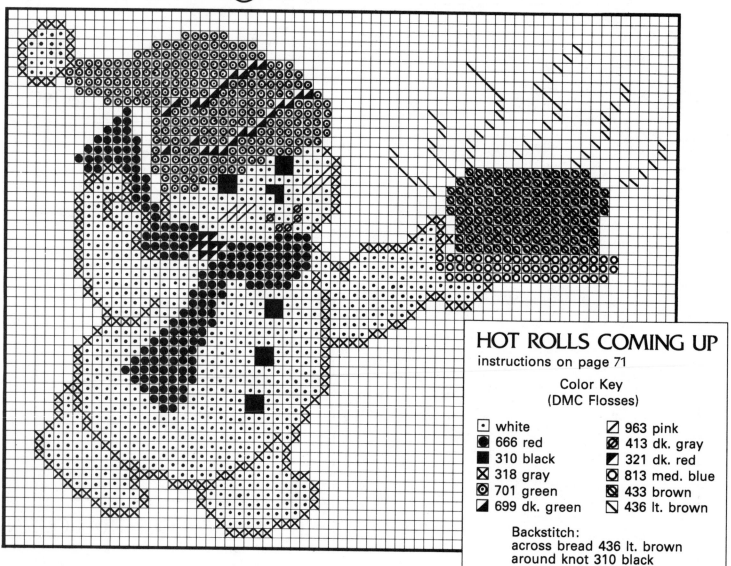

HOT ROLLS COMING UP
instructions on page 71

Color Key
(DMC Flosses)

⊡ white		◪ 963 pink	
◉ 666 red		◙ 413 dk. gray	
■ 310 black		◪ 321 dk. red	
☒ 318 gray		◎ 813 med. blue	
◉ 701 green		◙ 433 brown	
◪ 699 dk. green		◩ 436 lt. brown	

Backstitch:
across bread 436 lt. brown
around knot 310 black

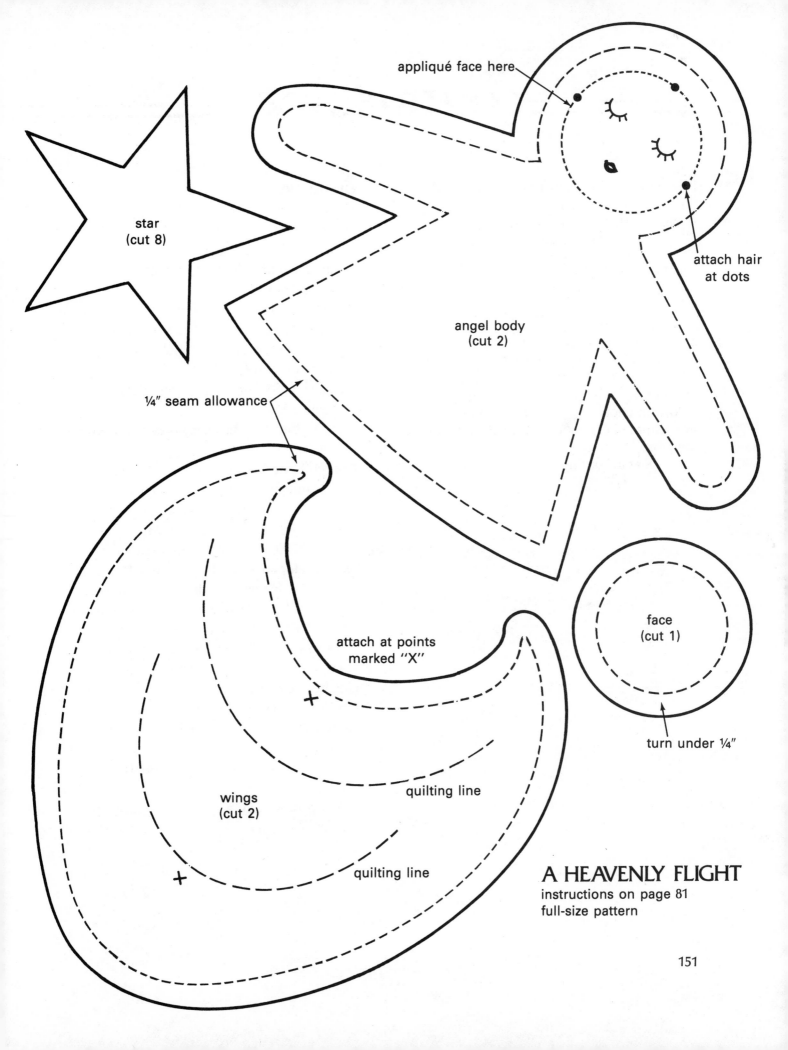

star
(cut 8)

appliqué face here

attach hair
at dots

angel body
(cut 2)

¼" seam allowance

face
(cut 1)

turn under ¼"

attach at points
marked "X"

wings
(cut 2)

quilting line

quilting line

A HEAVENLY FLIGHT
instructions on page 81
full-size pattern

151

CONTRIBUTORS

Production Editor: Annette Thompson
Editorial Assistant: Patty Howdon
Photo Stylist: Linda M. Stewart
Design: Viola Andrycich
Cover Photograph: Beth Maynor
Art: Don Smith, David Morrison
Production: Jerry Higdon

Special thanks to Maura Kennedy for her help in the planning stages of this book, and to Susan Payne, Creative Foods Editor at *Decorating & Craft Ideas*. Thanks also to the following people from *Southern Living*: Jean Wickstrom Liles, Foods Editor; Beverly Morrow, Foods Photo Stylist; and Vann Cleveland, Director of Photography.

DESIGNERS:

Dorinda Beaumont, basketweave placemats 36, metallic needlepoint 69.

Diane Brakefield, crewel ornament 50, sewing basket 60.

Robin Cangialosi, block prints 75.

Candace Conard, mantel arrangement 1.

John and Peggy Cranston, nutty critter ornaments 66 and 67.

Inez Crimmins, Brazilian embroidery ornaments 20.

Rita Martinez de Blake, painted bread dough nativity, bottom 65.

George L. de Victoria, pine cone wreath 26.

Jean Hafeman, lights in punchbowl 17 and title page, decoupage purse 51.

Dora Hooks, greenery cluster 23, ginkgo flowers 30, living ivy wreath 36.

Maxine Hopping, tortilla flowers 14.

Patricia J. Horton, powder puff ornaments 32, crochet wreath 32, ribbon hair clips 52, Christmas journal 55, cross-stitch breadwarmer 71, lady's travel accessories 76, man's travel accessories 78.

Elizabeth Lindley Jones, tartan angel 86.

Jan Kirkpatrick, Victorian ornaments 43.

Steve Logan, paper cardinals 31, stamped gift wrap 70.

Posey Baker Lough, ribbon bows 10 and 11, rope horses 80.

Jeanette B. McCay and Hanna Franz, "hibiscus" pine cone wreath 27.